Pastor Moe's book is really about transformation—from the inside out. If we are honest most of us have been or should be asked that difficult and revealing question, "Will I ever be happy?" This book is a potent reminder that we have to give ourselves, our families, our jobs, and our church BACK to God. He and He alone has to be the fuel for whatever He has placed us here to do. Our ideas, plans, or processes don't belong to us.

Moe's journey is a powerful example of one man's willingness to be "dealt with" and molded by a loving and sovereign God. The impact has reached many, including but not limited to the remarkable disciples at the Light of Christ Church. The impact for me is more personal; in the sharing of his transformative journey, Moe has challenged me to be bolder in my surrender and willingness to give the church and "my" ministry back to God—the one who gave it to me in the first place.

Thank you, Linda, for asking that tough question, and thank you, Moe, for being brave enough to answer—and for the subsequent willingness to share the journey in finding true happiness through your relationship with our loving Heavenly Father and the power of the Holy Spirit.

PASTOR ERIC MEISSNER
Trinity Lutheran Church, Avoca, IA

I can see that Pastor Moe had faith in our Lord and Savior Jesus Christ in wanting to serve others. God's timing is not always our timing, but Pastor Moe never gave up, even though it took nineteen years to get a church building. My late parents, Rev. James and Vera Dingman, prayed for seventeen years to have a children's home and their faith never wavered. God has blessed Sunshine Acres Children's Home more than I ever dreamed. Today, we have eight beautiful homes and we care for over eighty children and we are still growing. Since the home was started in 1954, we have cared for almost 2,000 children without state and federal money and we do not get paid for our children. It is truly a "Miracle in the Desert." Pastor Moe was encouraged by my parents' faith in God to meet all of Sunshine Acres Children's Home needs. As you read Pastor Moe's book, you will be inspired to see how God has worked through every obstacle while he kept the faith to fulfill his dream.

CAROL L. WHITWORTH
President and CEO, Sunshine Acres Children's Home, Mesa, AZ

I could write a book about the number of ways this book resonates with me. For the past five-and-a-half years, I've had the privilege of working full time to see Jesus' John 17 prayer answered in my city of Tucson. Moe's journey took him across the wide expanse of the beautiful body of Christ, from Lutheran to Assembly of God, and humility is the only road that can accommodate that journey. As Bill Hybels likes to say, "Armed with enough humility, we can learn from anybody." And as Moe so beautifully describes, when we truly follow the one who "came not be served, but to serve," not only does the world around us benefit, but so do we. Thanks, Moe, for so powerfully telling your compelling story!

DAVID DRUM
Church Domain Director, 4Tucson, Tucson, AZ
Author, *Jesus' Surprising Strategy: A mandate and a means for city transformation*

I never imagined that answering God's call would lead to a career filled with passion and purpose. I had no idea that God could use me, a full-time mom, to make such an impact in His kingdom. Talk about equipping the called rather than calling the equipped! But that is exactly what happened and my life has been so abundantly blessed in the process. I hope you take that away from reading Pastor Moe's inspiring story. We have spent many hours over the years talking about the miracles we see every day as we do our best to live our lives following in Jesus' footsteps. Trust me when I say that every one of you can make a difference when you follow where the Spirit leads. May this book encourage you to take that first step.

JANINE SKINNER
Development Advisor, Feed My Starving Children, Mesa, AZ

When I was in college, my marketing instructor would constantly challenge my class with one question: "Can you give me a practical example?" What he was driving at was, "If your theory doesn't produce anything in the real world, what good is it?" That question has stuck with me throughout the years—and this book provides not just one, but multiple practical examples of the Spirit of God at work in the lives of those who have been called to carry out the ministry. This is not a theory; this is the truth. At the end of the day, we need less talk and more walk. Thank you, Pastor Moe, for this practical example.

TODD MATCHETT
Lead Pastor, Living Hope Church, Merriville, IN

I am excited that the readers of this book are going to discover a new way that is not new at all—to live as joy-filled disciples of Christ who are led by the Holy Spirit. You will hear a clear challenge to let Jesus be Lord of His church. Moe will inspire you as he teaches you how he learned to let go of control of the church he served and let Jesus revitalize their ministry. This book is filled with stories of people who were set on fire for Christ when they learned how to listen to His voice. Thank you, Pastor Moe Redding, for letting us share your journey of learning to let Holy Spirit lead you.

PASTOR STEVE BERGESON
Shepherd of the Hills Church, Fountain Hills, AZ.

"We are not called to be great pastors, whatever that means. We are called to become great servants as we are discipled by the greatest Servant of all through the pure power of the Holy Spirit." This quote from Pastor Moe's book is a powerful summary of all that the Lord has done with Moe, to him, through him, and sometimes in spite of him. This is a tremendous insight to the power of the Holy Spirit and a humble recognition that the congregations we serve belong to Jesus. Our best and highest calling is simply to desire each day to be faithful servants of His. As a commentary on American Christianity, this book is revolutionary and inspiring—and as a call to pastors, it is freedom from the demands of a worldly view of God's Church. I recommend this to everyone who seeks the freedom and power of the Spirit of the living God.

MARK VANDER TUIG
Service Coordinator, Lutheran Congregations in Mission for Christ

Pastor Redding has written a beautiful account of how he and the congregation he serves discovered what it means to die to one's own pride and plans in order to daily listen to the Lord to learn His plan. We catch the sense of adventure they have experienced as the Lord uses them to fulfill His purpose in working miracles and transforming lives. Whether a pastor or church member, the reader can't help but hunger for the same kind of walk with the Lord. Pastor Redding shows us so clearly that following Jesus' guidance day-by-day and hour-by-hour makes all the difference in the world between ministry as usual and ministry modeled after the book of Acts.

PASTOR CAROL PETERS
Retired Associate Pastor,
La Casa de Cristo Lutheran Church, Scottsdale, AZ

Jesus told us that greatness is learning to serve others. In this book, Moe tells about how Jesus changed his idea of what a pastor should be doing and challenged him to simplify the message. He tells story after story about how Jesus changed the hearts of others by teaching them the joy of serving. Jesus will change your life too if you will focus on loving him and serving others.

PASTOR PAUL WITKOP
Light in the Desert Church, Cave Creek, AZ

Too many people start out as a missionary for Jesus and end up being nothing more than a mercenary! It happens to pastors and laypeople alike. A missionary listens to the Spirit and does what God wants. A mercenary does what is expected or beneficial and protective of themselves. This journey with Pastor Moe shares his journey and how he went from missionary to mercenary AND his journey back! It is something we all need to read and then apply to our own journey with Jesus.

PASTOR ANDREW GARMAN
Founding Pastor, La Casa de Cristo Lutheran Church, Scottsdale, AZ

PURE POWER!

Spirit-led Ministry for Spirit-starved People

MOE REDDING
WITH ADAM COLWELL

Adam Colwell's
writeworks

Adam Colwell's WriteWorks Publishing
Adam Colwell's WriteWorks LLC, Tucson, AZ

Printed in the United States of America

Contributed to and edited by Adam Colwell
Cover design by Jaime Anaya
Interior design and typesetting by Katherine Lloyd, The DESK

ISBN: 978-0-9982593-5-2
eBook ISBN: 978-0-9982593-6-9

Dedication
All glory to our Heavenly Father.
We owe you everything.

ACKNOWLEDGEMENTS

To Linda, my beautiful bride: I can never thank you enough for sharing your life with me. Your encouragement, faith, patience, and love have helped me to be strong when my strength was failing. I praise Him for you! I love you, always.

To my children, Elijah, Wade, Micah, and Noelle: You will never know what a blessing you are to me! One of the greatest privileges in my life is being your earthly father. Keep your eyes on Jesus. He has incredible plans for your lives. He will use you to love and encourage so many people! Stay with Him; He has all the details already worked out. Your mother and I are excited to see what He has next for each of you. Remember, when you get all big and grown up … don't forget to visit from time to time!

To my mother, Beverley: Your faith in our Heavenly Father, your hope during the toughest times, your encouragement of me, and your commitment to seeing the absolute best in everyone is beyond inspiring. You are a model of the godly life, and I glorify our Father in Heaven for you! I love you so much! Can't you hear Dad and all those who have gone before us shouting encouragement to us from Heaven?

To my church family at Light of Christ: Thank you for your love for Jesus and patience with me! I wouldn't trade our journey for the world. I'm very excited to see what the Father has next for us.

To my in-laws, Javier and JoAnn: Thank you for Linda! Thank you for your encouragement throughout our life together. You have always been there for us. We thank God for you and love you!

To my siblings, Ted, Ione, and Richard: Thank you for all the wonderful memories growing up. Isn't God good to us! Who knew He would bless us with such incredible lives and families? I love you.

To Adam Colwell: Thank you for joining me in this project. You have made this a wonderful process. It has truly been a joy working with you!

FOREWORD

There are few men that I have met in my 63 years of ministry that I felt had such a tender heart for God and His work as Pastor Moe Redding. When I first met him, he was on a quest to know God and to know God's heart. It was a quest that he was on personally, but one on which he had also brought along his entire church. On this quest, I saw him bring scores of people to the Dream Center to learn what an expression of the body of Christ, beyond denominations, could look like. In fact, his church was one of the very first to support the work of the Dream Center and to touch my heart in doing so.

I've found that it's the deepest desire of most pastors to want their congregations to not only know the Bible, but also to know how to turn what's in the Bible into practical and world-changing actions. As Pastor Moe's church began to do food and clothing drives, and then rally together to take it to the hardest hit and most poverty stricken areas of our city, I have no doubt that their pastor—and God—rejoiced to see a church do just that.

When I learned that Pastor Moe had written *Pure Power!* I was thrilled and I thought, "There could not have been a more relevant time for the body of Christ to get its hands on this book than right now." Pastor Moe writes in this wonderful book that I played an inspirational role in his life. But what he didn't write is that all along the way, he was encouraging me, too! I treasure the letters he wrote to me telling me of his quest and of his journey, and through them I felt I was right there with him—as you will, too, as you read this book.

In *Pure Power!* Pastor Moe moves the reader along the sometimes raw and real journey that many pastors take through ministry—the calling, the doubts, the setbacks, the questions, the balancing of occupation with family—and how he came to make a dramatic turnaround that saved and revolutionized his own life and calling to make disciples. Along his journey, Pastor Moe was reminded that ministry leadership can and should be more than merely being overworked and overwhelmed, because it really doesn't even belong to "us," but rather to Jesus.

He details a pivotal story involving his own church board of directors where huge changes were made to how all of the administrative and ministry departments were going to be run. Much of it would now be out of his hands! Many pastors would have seen the changes as a deal breaker and a "sign from God" that it was time for them to move on. But Pastor Moe saw it as a launching point and as a word from the Lord to change the course of his own ministry life. He took the path that emerged through those board changes, knowing that his ministry work, his relationships, and his very purpose would never be the same. What he found on that path rejuvenated and revitalized his ministry and changed the course of his church and his community.

With great insight and depth, Pastor Moe lays out a plan and a roadmap that many pastors in similar situations can follow. And which of us hasn't been in a similar situation? I found his insight into the challenges that we all face, as well as the tools he sets forth, to be timeless in their ability to change our ministry lives and the fruit of our ministries in a way that glorifies God and rejuvenates our souls.

This book is a celebration of our pastoral quest to better know and serve God. It's a proclamation and a voice crying loudly for all of the leaders of the body to rally around our central quest of humility and to leave a legacy pointing toward Jesus Christ, not toward ourselves. As pastors and caretakers of people, it's so very easy for us to get tied down to the day-to--day seemingly mundane things that perhaps really do need to be done, but not always by us. God, who was so faithful to call us, is equally faithful to shake up our world when we've allowed our "ministry business" to make us stray from His very own heart. It's in these moments that, as Pastor Moe shares, we so desperately need our first love in the ministry to be ignited again. Yes, our first "dolphin miracle," which was never intended to be a onetime thing but was intended to remain throughout the course of our entire ministry life and to be handed off and passed on to generations beyond us.

Pastors, are you tired? Burdened? Questioning the call? Wondering where the miracles are? Friend, I encourage you, as Pastor Moe did, take the principles and the strategies set forth in this book and put them to work in your own life. If you do, I know God will do a work in you that he's so obviously done in Pastor Moe's life, and in my own life, too—a work that stands the test of time, of culture, of change, and of uncertainty. A work that stands at the end of time to hear those words we are all longing for. "Well done, good and faithful servant." Well done.

Pastor Tommy Barnett
Senior Pastor, Phoenix First Assembly of God, Phoenix, AZ

Chapter 1

Many are the plans in the mind of a man,
but it is the purpose of the Lord that will stand.
PROVERBS 19:21

When my wife and God conspired against me, each one told me something I didn't expect and certainly didn't want to admit. But both said precisely what I needed to hear.

My life and ministry have never been the same.

It happened the night I was standing in the kitchen of my home in Chandler, Arizona, a prominent suburb of Phoenix that, back in the year 2000, was one of the fastest growing areas in the southwestern United States. That was important to me, because as a pastor I was in a race with many other pastors to be the first one to build and establish a megachurch in this sunny desert paradise; a church that would bring me prestige, prominence, and prosperity.

Like any other entrepreneurial pastor, I had a strategic plan to pull off my goal to hit the minimum Sunday morning service attendance threshold of one thousand people within four years. I hadn't consulted with God about this plan, but why should I? After all, the Lord wanted the pews filled. That's what the Great Commission is all about, right? In order to create a church that I thought God would be proud to call His own, we needed as many people as possible—and we absolutely had to be first. There was no way I could allow somebody else to claim the people I felt were rightfully mine.

But there was a problem. I was losing the race. One obstacle after another had thwarted my plan, and nothing was going to happen on my supposedly reasonable timeframe. I didn't show my frustration; I was adept at going behind the pulpit every Sunday and putting on the necessary performance. I thought the messages were powerful, and yet very little transformation was happening in our people. Worse, I knew something was deeply wrong with me! I was depressed to the point of utter misery, and right there, standing in my kitchen, I was pretty sure I knew why.

Either she was going to speak the truth in love, or we'd be leaving our church, packing up our house, and trekking back down Interstate 10 to go to college, go into massive debt in the process, and more than likely realize later that med school wasn't the answer on my quest for "happiness."

My wife, Linda, was over by the sink and I was sitting on a stool next to the counter. She was working and I was pondering. My father was a doctor, my mother a nurse, and Linda's and my previous home of Tucson had a fine university with a world-class medical school. Frustrated with everything happening in my ministry, I hinted that perhaps I should consider a change of vocation.

Then I asked her, "Where do you think we are going to be one year from now?"

"I think we'll be back at the University of Arizona, in an apartment with our boys as you go back to school," she said. There was no sarcasm. No sharpness to her tone. Just utter discouragement.

I plodded forward. "Maybe I've missed my calling. Maybe I'm not supposed to be a pastor, and the ministry was just an emotional thing for me. Maybe it's God's will that I should be a doctor. Maybe that's why I'm not happy."

Linda turned and looked at me. She didn't shake her head, but she didn't have to. The expression on her face, a disheartening mix of exasperation and pity, spoke volumes.

"Moe, I don't know if you're ever going to be happy."

Linda is a woman who tells it like it is. It was part of what attracted her to me back when we started dating in 1986. She was a part-time student at a community college, determinedly working her way through school with no monetary assistance other than what she earned on her own. I was just the opposite, a full-time student at the university pursuing my degree in religious studies (after switching my major from biology) and getting full financial help from my parents. On our first date she acted like she was going to shove a piece of pizza in my face. I told her, "I dare you." So she did. I tumbled out of the booth in a failed attempt at avoiding the pizza, looked up at her, and thought, "That's the girl for me!"

We are both very headstrong, so it's no surprise that the first year of our marriage was a full-on donnybrook as we both jockeyed for control. This conflict was caused in part by my youthful male suspicion as she spent late hours away from me at her job. The monster of distrust grew until the Lord gave me a very simple thought at the end of our first year together: "Exactly how long do you think a person will stay with you whose integrity you are constantly questioning?" I confessed and repented of my distrust of my beautiful bride. I told her, "Please forgive me for questioning you. I am all in. You can trust me one hundred percent, and I will do the same. No more suspicion and no more questions. I love you and I'm sorry." As we grew closer over time and developed the increased maturity that comes with age and growing in our relationships with God, we became a couple characterized by trust, mutual respect, and healthy give-and-take.

Still, her statement in the kitchen was completely unanticipated. I think she realized our family was at a vital turning point. Either she was going to speak the truth in love, or we'd be leaving our church, packing up our house, and trekking back down Interstate 10 to go to college, go into massive debt in the process, and more than likely realize later that med school wasn't the answer on my quest for "happiness."

Whacked by her words, I stumbled out of the kitchen and trod around the corner and up the stairs to the bedroom where I went inside, closed the door, flopped onto the bed, and hugged my pillow. *Why did she say that?* I mused. *How could she be so unsupportive?* I was wounded, but as I laid there and prayed, the Holy Spirit began to show me that Linda wasn't threatening me, nor was she being invalidating. She was simply stating a fact from her perspective. The sadness in her eyes also made me realize that this wasn't only about me—I was going to drag her and our eight-month-old twin boys along for the ride. So if I was going to leave the ministry, I had to be absolutely certain that it was really what God wanted me to do.

As I continued praying, another truth came to the fore. I recalled how I had been on fire for God as a college student, filled with the Holy Spirit and up early every morning before going off to class to spend time in His Word. I realized each day was a gift from the Lord. I was also a minister's assistant at a church, helping out with the choir and leading the worship service. I was serving, receiving tons of affirmation, loving every moment of it and thanking our Father for it.

I had also been front and center for a miracle from the Lord. It was the last day of a weeklong sailboat trip with our college age youth group. We left from Los Angeles and sailed to Catalina Island. It was an incredible time just to slow down, immerse myself in Bible study, get to know a lot of other kids, and relax in some of the nicest weather on the planet. The only problem was that we had not seen any marine life! Well, I shouldn't say that. There was an old seal that limped by one day. I'm not sure, but it looked like he had an oxygen tank and was wearing a flotation device. Needless to say, I had hoped for more.

So I was up in the bow of the boat spending time in prayer. I thanked the Lord for the week, though I did mention how it would have been nice to see more marine life. I opened my eyes, looked out to the horizon, and saw a dolphin jump! Then three jumped—then six. Next thing I know, a whole group of dolphins were swimming alongside our sailboat. They seemed to ignore all the other boats around us, but they had us completely surrounded!

We leaned over the side of the boat and touched them. More arrived in droves and before long there had to be over one hundred dolphins;

they were everywhere! It was mind boggling! They stayed with us, jumping and playing around the sailboat, for at least fifteen minutes. Everyone was astonished. I was overwhelmed. All I said, over and over again, was, "Thank you, Father. I love you, Father."

When I returned home I took out a sheet of paper and wrote on it, "Remember the dolphins. Do you know how much our Father loves you? Live for Him!" I taped it to my wall.

I was so excited to serve the Lord! *If I'm on fire like this*, I thought near the end of my senior year in college, *imagine how much I'm going to love the Lord after going to seminary?* But that was before I went to a mainline denominational seminary to be trained to become a "professional" pastor. Here is a fact that astonishes many people: at no time during those four years in seminary did anyone ever ask me about my relationship with Jesus Christ. Not once! I recall hearing a liturgical priest later say, "When I went to seminary, they taught us how to take the Bible apart. But now I realize the Bible takes me apart." Sure enough, I had stopped reading the Bible. I stopped listening to Jesus. I stopped submitting to Him! I blamed the seminary, not realizing then that it was my own fault. I got distracted and neglected my relationship with the Lord. In the years since, I had never recovered that earlier passion.

I had given my life to Jesus, but never *my ministry.*
For the first time in my life, I gave up control
of the ministry to the Lord.

So I knew I was no longer on fire—at least, not for the things that mattered to God. I was, however, well versed in the intricacies of church growth and megachurch management and had attended conference after conference on the subject. But Jesus? The Holy Spirit? His miracles? I'd forgotten the dolphins. I'd become a personification of the church in Leodicea in Revelation 3. I'd lost my first love of Christ. My lukewarm pot of water was sitting on the stove top with the burner completely off. No Holy Spirit fire here! Truth be told, I was getting downright cold, a dead pool. But I did spend a lot of time complaining to the Lord about my situation with very little, if any, time given to thanking and praising Him for all His blessings each and every day. I wonder: if I had only complained to the Lord on that sailboat without also thanking Him, would He have sent the dolphins? How many miracles are connected with a thankful heart? Remember, only the leper who was healed and then returned to give thanks to Jesus was declared "well." (Luke 17:19)

Somehow I thought no one else knew of the lukewarm state of my soul, but Linda shattered that misperception.

I was at a point of decision, in the throes of a Holy Spirit intervention that night on my bed. My spirit grieved and cried out to God. *Lord, you have got to show me how to come back from this. I don't love you the way I used to. I don't love my family the way I'm supposed to. I don't love the lost; I don't love the church.* Fresh tears moistened my pillow. *If being a doctor is what you'd have me to do, God, I'll do it; but I'd like to stay in the ministry if at all possible. But Lord, you have to show me how to come back or move me out, because I can't keep doing this.*

An interesting thing happens when you get to the end of your rope— you stop! I was hanging there too weak to climb back up and too afraid to let go and plunge into the abyss. I needed to be rescued, and my deliverance came.

It was a voice, His voice, booming in my mind.

"Moe, are you going to give me back my church?"

God had posed a strong but simple "yes" or "no" question, and He wanted an answer. Without hesitation, I responded.

"Lord, it is yours."

Two things happened in that moment. First, I realized my problem had nothing to do with my circumstances and everything to do with my heart—and, more specifically, my ego. I had sunk so low because I wasn't working to bring people to God; I was bringing them to myself! You can't have "megachurch" without "me," right? It was clear that my ego was more than clouding my vision; it was blinding me. It was also destroying me. I had given my life to Jesus, but never *my ministry*. For the first time in my life, I gave up control of the ministry to the Lord. "It's all yours." I repeated. "Build this ministry as big or as small as you want, but I promise you this: from now on, it will be all about you."

With the declaration of that promise to Him, the second thing happened: I immediately experienced a surge of joy—pure, uninhibited, and not felt in years—sweep through my spirit. I sensed God was proud of me, and not only did I know I was restored to Him, but I was convinced the ministry was going to be different from that point on.

There was no way to know then the radical changes the Lord had in store for us all.

This book is for people in ministry who truly want to honor and serve the Lord, but you are starting to question your call. Now, it could be that He has something else for you. If so, follow the leading of the Holy Spirit and pursue that vocation. He will use you mightily there. But there might be another reason for your discontent. Perhaps, if you're like me, you are meant to be in the ministry you're in now, but you're *doing it wrong*. Praise God! The first step to a new life is admitting the problem. Know this: our Father loves you. He loves you enough to discipline you. What you consider burnout may actually be Him withholding peace and joy in an attempt to get your attention. You need to hear nothing I say and everything He says. Perhaps something in these pages will ignite your spirit and encourage you to become the unique child of God He created you to be. I hope so. God gets the glory when you become uniquely you— and the ministry you serve will never be the same.

I am sure my story is similar to many others in ministry. I started seminary in the strength of and reliance upon the Holy Spirit, wanting to serve Jesus, but slowly I made it about me. By the time I became a pastor, I was no longer seeking the praise that comes from God, but rather the accolades of man. I would have been right at home when Jesus said, "How can you believe, when you receive glory from one another and do not seek the glory that comes from the only God?" (John 5:44)

Jesus refused people's praise. He said quite clearly, "I do not receive glory from people." (John 5:41) Simply put, He did not let people's praise or criticism control Him in any way. Instead, He focused on obedience to His Father, and His Father rewarded Him with glory, the glory that comes from the only God. I believe that is what joy is: our Father's reward for obedience. People cannot give us this joy. It is our Father whispering to our souls, "I am proud of you. Well done!" It is fruit of the Spirit and only comes from God.

Look at the connection between obedience, love, and joy in this teaching from our Lord. He said, "If you keep my commandments, you will abide in my love, just as I have kept my Father's commandments and abide in his love. These things I have spoken to you, that my joy may be in you, and that your joy may be full." (John 15:10-11) Jesus was obedient, abided in our Father's love, and His Father gave Him joy. He desires that same joy for us! I had been disobedient, had not abided in His love, and He had withheld His joy. I gave the Lord back His ministry and my life, and He gave me back His joy! Praise be to God, for the joy of the Lord is my strength (Nehemiah 8:10).

The morning after my wife and my Lord dealt with me, I rose early and read the Bible, once again on fire and blazing. The subject of moving or medical school never came up again. I knew what God wanted— and so did Linda. That Sunday at church, I preached with a power and freedom that was a visible manifestation of the fresh renewal of my relationship with our Heavenly Father. The Spirit's power was back and burning! Those who were there that morning said later that they knew something was different about me—it was clear that something had changed within.

And it had. But this was only the beginning. There was still so very much to burn away inside of Moe Redding.

⚜

That was sixteen years ago, and what has happened in my life since then as a pastor and as a child of God as well as in the life of His congregation is miraculous. Light of Christ Church, "A Place to Belong," indeed fulfilled a building program—but it was on His timetable, happened through His maneuverings, and it achieved His purposes. We are a church that first listens to Jesus, is then Spirit-led, and then follows with servant ministries founded and operated on the fact that, as we serve the least in the world, we are actually serving Jesus. (Matthew 25:40) God has shown us that the key to life is to give our lives away, first to the Lord and then to others. This relentless focus on listening to Jesus and serving others has resulted in real-life stories of God's life-altering power that you will read through the testimonies of the very people He has used and blessed to His glory.

We realize that Light of Christ is a very small part of God's worldwide ministry, and we constantly ask for the Holy Spirit's wisdom to discern the work He has given us to do. Through insight given by God, and the refining fire of the Holy Spirit over the last two decades, we have identified five principles— **repent, rededicate, restructure, refocus, and rejoice**—that I will detail throughout our story and wholeheartedly believe will result in God's ministers and His people discovering the unique purpose and destiny He has for each one of us. We now have a different vision that is not about church growth, but is primarily about the heart of the ministry leader and his or her spiritual growth, who then leads by example.

Praise be to God we have the witness of His first disciples!
We can learn from them. There are also many sold out followers
of Jesus in our world today who are shining examples for all of us
of true discipleship—if we have the *humility and desire to learn.*

I believe God has placed a dream in the heart of every believer to reach out and serve others. This starts with what Jesus says is the only necessary thing: listening to Him. As we **listen to the Lord** and draw close to Him, He will lead us in His perfect love to serve others and help us discover what it means to be **true disciples** of Christ.

In the Great Commission, our Lord commanded His disciples to make disciples of all nations (Matthew 28: 16-20). This was their job then—and it is our job now. However, we may have overlooked a massive truth. I know I did. When Jesus gave this command, He was talking to His core group of men; eleven guys. This was not a command for thousands. Why? These eleven were actual, fully-committed followers of His. He knew it. They knew it. Making disciples was going to be relatively easy for them: simply teach others what they were learning. However, if they were disciples in *name only*, making actual disciples of Jesus was going to be next to impossible. They wouldn't have any idea what they were talking about!

The situation is precisely the same today. Before I begin asking *how* to make disciples, I need to address the most basic question: am I, in fact a disciple of Jesus? Would I be included in that small group of sold out, fully-committed followers of Christ—and is there any way to know for sure?

Praise be to God we have the witness of His first disciples! We can learn from them. There are also many sold out followers of Jesus in our world today who are shining examples for all of us of true discipleship—if we have the *humility and desire to learn.* The Lord will give us eyes to see them and hearts to learn from them. The Holy Spirit will bring them to us and use their incredible faith to ignite our faith! All glory to God!

Finally, I believe the Lord wants us to learn that *all* ministry belongs to God. He owns it. It never belonged to us. This was never about us. It was always about Him. Ministry is not an ego thing, but an obedience thing; die to self and follow Jesus. He chose us to be a small part of what He is doing, but He gets all of the glory. That's the deal. As we allow God to set us free—from ego, from expectation, from competing against each other, from the numbers game, from "professionalism"—He'll slow us down and use us to serve others. Instead of looking for blessing, we will each *become the unique blessing* we are created to be, and so will His ministry.

It all began for me that night when I repented and gave the Lord's church back to Him and started my walk as His disciple; a follower, not a leader. I invite you now to join me as I share how the Lord persistently chiseled away at me from that point forward—piece by piece, layer by layer in an all-encompassing battle against my ego—to learn to listen to God, decrease so He may increase, and be positioned to help Light of Christ truly become His ministry, for His glory! As awesome as the dolphins were, that miracle paled in comparison to what the Lord had in store.

Chapter 2

Do nothing from selfish ambition or conceit, but in humility
count others more significant than yourselves.
PHILIPPIANS 2:3

I don't recall exactly how I first found out about Pastor Tommy Barnett and Phoenix First Assembly of God church, since the denomination and tradition I came out of are both radically different than theirs. However, in the months after I repented and rededicated my life and ministry to the Lord, I knew without question that I needed help. I realized that the Lord had to lead me to others who knew what being a disciple of Jesus is all about, as well as to discover what a discipling, servant congregation looked like. I had no idea.

But the more I researched Pastor Barnett, his church, and an outreach it pioneered called the Dream Center, the more I found that I liked. Barnett and his son Matthew launched the Dream Center in Los Angeles in September 1994 as a home missions project. Beginning with a church averaging fewer than fifty people on a Sunday morning, Dream Center today serves tens of thousands of people per month and has spawned similar outreaches nationwide, including one in Phoenix itself. It rescues and rehabilitates people from addictions, homelessness, and abuse, including victims of human trafficking, gang members, unwed mothers, and at-risk youth, as well as feeding the hungry and needy.

Pastor Barnett said the key to servant ministry such as this was to "find a need and fill it, find a hurt and heal it." I loved that! Then I became aware that Phoenix First offered a discipleship service every Wednesday night. Perfect! We didn't have midweek services at Light of Christ, so I decided to go—and I couldn't wait to hear Pastor Barnett in person. I made the forty-five minute drive north from Chandler and took my seat in the huge auditorium. The service commenced with upbeat worship music, with those in attendance engaging in enthusiastic praise. Then people were asked to come forward for prayer as we prayed with each other and for each other. Both experiences were new to me, and I was intrigued with the joy, love, and freedom everyone seemed to have.

Then Pastor Barnett came to the podium and made an announcement that stopped the powerful worship experience in its tracks, at least for me. "Ninety-five percent of the time, I preach every service here," he said. "But not tonight."

What! He wasn't going to speak?

My heart sank and my frustration rose. I drove all this way to hear Pastor Barnett preach, not someone else. I was a senior pastor, after all; I wanted to be discipled by Barnett himself, not one of his associates! I considered getting up and leaving right then and there, but my pride also kept me planted where I was. I didn't want to embarrass the guest speaker, whoever he was—or myself. It wasn't like anyone else was leaving anyway, though I was certain everyone shared my disappointment.

As I stewed, Pastor Barnett continued. "Let me introduce Pastor Todd. He has been on our staff for ten years and I asked him to bring the Word of God to us tonight. Todd, come and share what the Lord has put on your heart for us this evening."

And up he came—this young guy who couldn't have been more than thirty years of age. He was huge, a Mr. Universe-type, and was practically busting out of his suit.

I was insulted. *What's this muscle head got to say that I need to hear?*

He started preaching about Jesus walking on the water from John 6.

"When evening came, his disciples went down to the sea, got into a boat, and started across the sea to Capernaum. It was now dark, and Jesus had not yet come to them. The sea became rough because a strong wind was blowing. When they had rowed about three or four miles, they saw Jesus walking on the sea and coming near the boat, and they were frightened. But he said to them, 'It is I; do not be afraid.' Then they were glad to take him into the boat, and immediately the boat was at the land to which they were going." (John 6:16-21)

Pastor Todd emphasized neither Christ's aqueous trek nor His words of comfort. Instead, he focused on how the disciples kept rowing, foot after agonizing foot, despite the storm and the lack of their Lord's presence. He told of how they didn't quit, then emphasized, "If you shortcut the process, you shortcut the promise." He added, "Keep being faithful to do what God tells you to do. Keep rowing, don't ever quit, and you're going to see the miracle."

He spoke with an undeniable power and authority. I felt my ego take a deserved blow straight on the chin. *Oh my goodness,* I thought. *This guy's better than me!*

The Word the Holy Spirit poured through Pastor Todd that night has encouraged me to this very day. It is probably the sermon that comes to my mind more than any other in my entire life! But something impressed me even more that night. As Todd preached, Tommy Barnett was on the platform, sitting on the edge of his seat with his eyes riveted on the young man—and was cheering him on like the most encouraging head coach I'd ever seen! He held his open Bible in one hand so he could pump his fist with the other. "Yes!" "Oh, that's great!" "Praise God!" Pastor Barnett was not miked, but his thrilled voice echoed off the walls of the massive sanctuary. He shouted one word of encouragement after the other at his junior associate.

I'd never seen anything like that before! I knew pastors were called to encourage their ministry leaders, but not at the level I was witnessing. My eyes, ears, mind, and heart were in shock. I was amazed and utterly convicted. *Am I seeing what I am seeing?*

Then came the kicker. "I never knew my father," Pastor Todd said in closing. "He left when I was very young. I'm heading to Toronto to become a senior pastor there." He turned toward Barnett. "But before I go, I just want to thank you, Pastor Barnett, for the last ten years. You've given me love and encouragement." He began to cry. "You're my spiritual father."

Tommy Barnett rose, slowly walked over as he wiped away his own tears, and gave Todd a big bear hug. He released him, put his hand on his shoulder, and turned to us in the congregation. "How many of you know this young man is going to be used by God in mighty ways? We are already so proud of him, but we are praising God for what He's going to do next through Todd in Toronto. What a privilege that we got to be part of his life!"

I was in awe. It was mind-numbing. My head was spinning, but somehow I knew this kind of encouragement was absolutely of God. So were the tears! These men were *real*! They weren't playing some role or trying to project some image that might attract others to their ministries. The encouragement was real, the Holy Spirit power was real, the heartfelt thanks was real, the tears were spontaneous, and the love of our Heavenly Father in that room was overwhelming. It was all real! And the Lord slowly broke my heart with the knowledge that this is all He wanted from me: the *real* me!

The ministry God desired to grow through me needed the real me, not some bad copy of someone else and their ministry. God needs the *real you* to build the ministry He has planned for you.

As part of my seminary training, I spent a year as an intern with a congregation in Ohio. I learned a great deal that year, and the people were terrific. At my exit interview, my supervising pastor, Alan Dietz, said, "Moe, I don't know what your ministry is going to look like, but it's not going to look like what we have here." Because I am a sensitive soul, I immediately felt this was a criticism. *I can do this job!* I thought at the time. However, now I realize he was not criticizing me. He just knew that ministry didn't fit who I was, or who I am now, and he was right! It was the ministry the Lord had grown through him, but mine was going to be different because I am different. The ministry God desired to grow through me needed the real me, not some bad copy of someone else and their ministry. God needs the *real you* to build the ministry He has planned for you. That is the adventure He has prepared for you.

It didn't occur to me until much later that if my initial visit to Phoenix First Assembly had not occurred with Tommy Barnett on the "sidelines," I would never have seen his remarkable heart of encouragement, love, and support for Pastor Todd. If Tommy had preached, I can imagine myself taking plenty of notes and being inspired by his insights and encouraged to point people to Jesus. Who knows? I may not have returned, thinking I had learned everything I needed to learn. Instead, I was given a completely different vision of what a ministry leader can be—and all because Pastor Todd was in the spotlight, bringing a message I desperately needed to hear, literally cheered the whole way by Pastor Barnett, ending in a tearful embrace! The Lord works in mysterious ways.

As the days passed, I knew I had seen servant leadership personified in Pastor Tommy Barnett. I also realized that he was the kind of servant leader I wanted to be.

There was still so much to learn. Nevertheless, one thing was for sure. My reserved perception of a pastor—someone who behaved a certain way in order to project a certain image—was rocked to its core. I knew I could never go back. I wanted to be able to let it go like Pastor Barnett did, to burn with passion to encourage others. *That* was the pastor I wanted to be. More than that, it was the person I wanted to be; the real me! Now that I had a vision of what could be, it ruined me for anything else.

Pastor Barnett helped me to understand how essential it is to get a vision of what can be. He used this analogy: we all learn to ride a bike the same way. First, we need to see someone else riding a bike. We need a vision. Once we see that, especially if the person riding the bike isn't too impressive, something may ignite within our minds. "If that guy can ride a bike, then certainly I can learn!" It is that vision that gets me up on that bike and keeps me going through all the crashes and skinned knees. That vision ignites the faith in me to believe I am going to learn how to ride a bike. At some point, as long as I do not give up, I learn how to ride. Now it is no longer an issue of faith. Now I *know* how to ride a bike. But it all started with a vision.

Pastor Barnett gave me a vision of what Spirit-led and Spirit-fed ministry can be. I had no idea what the particulars were going to eventually look like for me. I only knew I could never go back. Would I keep my job? I decided to leave that up to the Lord.

I made two decisions then that were vital to my development as a ministry leader and as a follower of Jesus. First, I started attending the discipleship services every Wednesday night at Phoenix First Assembly. Yes, Pastor Barnett spoke each time from that point forward, but who was speaking was no longer as important to me as allowing the Lord to do whatever He wanted within me, to nurture the soil in my spirit that I sensed was growing something new, exciting and significant in my desire to be a true disciple of Jesus. Second, I started serving others by volunteering with Phoenix First Assembly's outreach to the poor that took place every Saturday morning. I wanted to be a servant without the pressure of leadership that came with my pastorate. It was just me and caring for people.

Well, not quite *just* me. On Saturdays, I was paired with Bill, an older gentleman who must've been in his mid-eighties and moved about one mile an hour. I mean, he was *slow*. He could barely walk, but he had a heart of gold. I later learned he had once been confined to a wheelchair before God healed him so that he could walk again. Bill was there every Saturday and was filled with so much love it seemed he was just ready to burst. The outreach was simple yet utterly profound. We showed up at the church at 8:00 a.m., and each duo was given food donated from grocery stores as well as some donated clothing. We were then dispatched to depressed areas throughout the valley, found a spot and set up tables to display the food and clothes, and then knocked on doors and invited people to come take what they needed. When they came to the tables, we engaged folks in conversation and talked to them about Jesus and His love. It was a gentle, compassionate process—and absolutely awesome.

At the Wednesday night services, I found Pastor Barnett to be utterly passionate for God but also a remarkably humble soul. He was not self-promoting in any way (I had friends who lived just a few miles away from his church and never even knew it existed). Instead, it was all about Jesus and, as Tommy often said, "becoming a miracle instead of looking and waiting for miracles." One of his cornerstone teachings is from the story of Elisha and the widow's olive oil from 2 Kings 4:1-7.

> "Now the wife of one of the sons of the prophets cried to Elisha, 'Your servant my husband is dead, and you know that your servant feared the Lord, but the creditor has come to take my two children to be his slaves.' And Elisha said to her, 'What shall I do for you? Tell me; what have you in the house?' And she said, 'Your servant has nothing in the house except a jar of oil.' Then he said, 'Go outside, borrow vessels from all your neighbors, empty vessels and not too few. Then go in and shut the door behind yourself and your sons and pour into all these vessels. And when one is full, set it aside.' So she went from him and shut the door behind herself and her sons. And as she poured they brought the vessels to her. When the vessels were full, she said to her son, 'Bring me another vessel.' And he said to her, 'There is not another.' Then the oil stopped flowing. She came and told the man of God, and he said, 'Go, sell the oil and pay your debts, and you and your sons can live on the rest.'"

From this story, Pastor Barnett says that the reason why so few ministries see miracles is because they are no longer bringing in empty vessels. Everyone is already full and wants to receive more instead of reaching out to truly hurting people (empty vessels) to pour the love of Jesus into them. He also says everything ministries need to experience miracles is already in their house; they don't need to look anywhere else. The empty vessels may be outside, but the jars of oil are inside. As leaders, we are to pray and seek God for discernment about *who is already here* to be a miraculous instrument of God's supernatural power and love, and is ready to take the next step in discipleship.

I fed upon his Spirit-powered insights of the Bible each week and quickly came to realize that my own inner transformation was going to indeed be an ongoing, long-term process. As Pastor Todd had said, there were not going to be any shortcuts.

I continued doing both the Wednesday and Saturday activities for over a year, and I was in full-on learning mode. One of the things Pastor Barnett said that I remember most is that "a servant church will always be relevant." That's really the heart of it, isn't it? If, as a ministry, we truly intend to serve and care for people, the Lord will always have ministry for us—and He will bless, empower, and provide for it! When we identify ourselves by a denomination, it is likely we resist change at all costs because we need to maintain the "brand." When we are programmatic, there's always a need to find the latest, greatest program, to improvise and improve, to keep the numbers up. But if the love of God compels us, and we sincerely want to care for people *for their sake*, and we pray, "Lord, bring us to hurting people, or bring them to us, and we will serve them," I believe the Lord answers that prayer in astonishing ways!

Occasionally no one came for worship.
This was disappointing, but we kept rowing.

The next thing to do was to apply what I was learning to what we did at Light of Christ. Step one was the launch of yearly, five-day-long missions trips to Mexico. My beautiful bride spearheaded and led this project, using her knowledge of the needs of the Mexican people gained from her upbringing in San Diego and many trips across the border into Tijuana. Using some of her connections there, we started taking as many as one hundred congregation members with us to Mexico to build homes. It was down and dirty work; no electrical tools could be used because there was no electricity where we went, so the eleven-by-twenty-two concrete slabs were mixed and poured from a wheelbarrow and the frame was put together with handsaws, hammers, and nails.

One of the first complaints we heard from neighbors back home was, "Why are you building homes in Mexico instead of your church building here?" Many of the complaints were from people tired of dealing with the dust blowing off our empty lot. Needless to say, we didn't mind the criticism. This was our first move out of the box to provide pure, simple service to the needy. The question then became, "How do we bring this servant heart with us back from Mexico into Suburban U.S.A.?"

The Holy Spirit led us to purchase a bus and begin a ministry in partnership with the La Mesita Transitional Housing (now Family Homeless Shelter) in Mesa, Arizona. Each Saturday we went to La Mesita with bread and other pastries donated by Paradise Bakery and some poster boards and crayons for the kids, and we connected with the residents at the center. All of these men and women were attempting to transition from a crisis living situation to stability and were in severe need. On Sunday, we returned with the bus and transported people to and from our morning worship services at Light of Christ. Occasionally no one came for worship. This was disappointing, but we kept rowing.

Sometimes we only saw a family or individual once; other occasions, several times. But it was wonderful, direct, servant ministry—and all these years later we still have families with us who first came to Light of Christ through that inaugural outreach ministry to our local community. The bus ministry continued for six years until we felt God bringing it to an end, which allowed us to give the bus away to an immigrant Ethiopian church in Peoria, Arizona who needed it for their children's ministry. The annual Mexico mission trips still continue today.

The start of the Mexico trips and bus ministry came about two years after repenting and rededicating my life to God and giving Him back His ministry at Light of Christ. The Spirit was blessing these ministries and pouring love, faith, and hope through me like never before. But I was still rowing and had a long way to go and a lot more to learn as the Lord continued to show me how to get out of my own way and, as Paul writes, "Do nothing from selfish ambition or conceit, but in humility count others more significant than yourselves." (Philippians 2:3)

Then the Lord brought to my attention some current superheroes of the faith, people with the same faith as the first disciples, and my comfortable American Christian worldview would never be the same again.

Chapter 3

Remember those who are in prison,
as though in prison with them …
HEBREWS 13:3A

The knowledge of these superheroes came to me through a Voice of the Martyrs magazine. It happened after one of the people we served at La Mesita ordered a starter kit for me as a gift. When it arrived, I set it aside for four months. One day, though, I glanced over at it and decided to take a look inside. As I read the articles provided of those past and present who were willing, and often did, give their very lives because of their love for Jesus and others, I began to weep. I learned that persecution in the Christian church, and the amazing level of love these people have for God and for others, is the norm—and was still happening in our modern day.

At a Voice of the Martyrs conference just a couple of years ago, "Brother John" (not his real name) told us what happened recently to "Brother Sam" in an Islamic country in the Middle East. Sam is absolutely on fire for the Lord. He wants everyone to know about Jesus, His love for them, and the new life He has for them. Sam's method is simple. He loads up his backpack with small New Testament Bibles and goes to businesses where he steps up to the counter, takes out a New Testament, and says, "This is the greatest gift you will ever receive. In it you will read about Jesus and His love for you. He died to save you from your sins. Please read this beautiful book and learn about Jesus."

Sam was about to depart his home for another day of witnessing when his friends pulled him aside. John told him, "Please stay away from the central part of the city. The Secret Police are focusing on that area." Sam simply stated, "I will go where I feel the Spirit leads me." With that, he walked away.

He did not return that night. Friends and family gathered to cry out to the Lord and pray for Sam's protection. The next day, a few went to the Secret Police headquarters and inquired about Sam. The police told them they did not have Sam in custody. The prayers continued and two days later Sam's family and friends returned to the jail. They pled with the officers, "Please. We don't care if you are torturing him. We simply need to know if he is alive." The officers responded, "We do not have this man in custody. If you come back, we will arrest you!"

Sam's family and friends gathered once more, but this time their prayers were filled with grief. They were convinced Sam had been killed because of his faith in Jesus and love for others. Two days later, John was outside working on his car. He glanced down the street and saw Sam walking toward him. "It was either Sam or his angel," John told us. It was Sam! Everyone surrounded him, praising God and crying tears of joy. Then they got angry. "Where have you been? Do you have any idea what you have put us through?"

"I appreciated your concern for me before I left," he said. "I knew you did not want me to go to that area of the city, but as I walked and listened to the Lord I was convinced that was precisely where He wanted me to go. So that is where I went. I began going into businesses, giving them Bibles, and telling them about Jesus and His love. Pretty soon the Secret Police arrived. They told me to leave the area or they would arrest me. I took my backpack and walked straight for two blocks, made a left and walked one block, made another left and walked two blocks, and began handing out Bibles in the same neighborhood."

Sam continued, "The Secret Police found me, arrested me, took me to jail, tossed my backpack in the corner, beat me up, and then threw me into a jail cell. I was full of fear, but I knew God was using me." He said that as he looked around the cell at the other prisoners, a thought came to him. "'I bet these men don't know anything about Jesus.' So I began telling them about Jesus." As men started accepting Jesus as Lord and Savior, Sam said the Secret Police were furious and beat him some more. "It didn't matter. I wanted everyone to know Jesus. After a few days, I realized that none of these men knew the songs we sing in church, so I began teaching them our songs of praise and love to Jesus. That really made the officers mad. The jail was turning into a church!"

Finally, Sam said the regional commander was called in. "They could not execute me without his approval. He met with me and told me, 'You will stop telling people about Jesus and leading these worship services in the jail. The only reason I am here is to execute you, which is precisely what I will order if you do not promise me you will stop telling others about Jesus.'"

Sam said he was quiet for a moment, and then looked at the commander. "'Not only will I not stop telling people about Jesus, but I am going to tell you about Jesus right now.' So I did. I told him how much Jesus loves him. That we are all sinners but Jesus died for sinners. I told him all he needed to do was ask Jesus into his heart, and our Lord would forgive him and heal him from all his sins, and he would be saved. When I finished, the commander took a piece of paper and wrote something on it. He handed it to me and said, 'This is my personal cell phone number. If any Secret Police ever bother you again, have them call me at any time of the day or night, and I will protect you. Take your backpack and Bibles, and go home.'"

This is the kind of faith I want to have! Stories like this were shared in magazine after magazine. It was true. This kind of faith and life actually exists! I exulted within. In Matthew 5:10, Jesus tells us "Blessed are those who are persecuted for righteousness' sake, for theirs is the kingdom of heaven." He also declared, "Blessed are those who hunger and thirst for righteousness, for they will be satisfied." (Matthew 5:6) That was me! I was hungrier for Him than at any time since I'd become a pastor. The Lord began revealing Himself to me in astonishing ways! I also started to understand that Christians are created for a life of daring adventure powered by the Holy Spirit as we serve Jesus and, if necessary, give up our lives for Him.

No wonder so many people are bored and entertainment-saturated in America today, even in congregations. They know there's more to life, a greater adventure to be lived. But they don't know the answer. Sadly, some ministries have bought into this trend, striving to *entertain* people instead of challenging them with these words of our Savior, which alone will lead to the truly adventurous life we are created to live:

"If anyone would come after me, let him deny himself and take up his cross daily and follow me. For whoever would save his life will lose it, but whoever loses his life for my sake will save it." (Luke 9:23-24)

Pastor Richard Wurmbrand, founder of Voice of the Martyrs, wrote in *Reaching Toward the Heights*, "There is no law that obliges Christians to be dull, lukewarm, [or] half-hearted. Christianity can be heroic. The right spelling of the word 'love' is S-A-C-R-I-F-I-C-E."

Through the Voice of the Martyrs, the Lord challenged me to give up more of my life and ministry to the Holy Spirit, trusting the Lord to lead the way. God was calling me outside of the darkness of selfishness, safety, and comfort into His life of light and service to others. The Shepherd's voice is proclaiming the same message to every one of His followers.

Jeff called me the next day. "I know I'm supposed to do something," he said. "I'm not sure yet what it is."

Take Jeff Pfingsten, for example. Before coming to Light of Christ, he had been away from church for ten years. Before that, he served as an usher at what he described as a strict, legalistic church. He said a "hoo-hah" broke out after he made a request for more ushers, which led to turmoil. The conflict angered him and he left, deciding that he wanted nothing more to do with organized religion. However, when he got married, his wife desired to go to church, and a friend told him about Light of Christ. They visited and decided to stay, but Jeff didn't want to be involved in ministry. He was still wounded by what had happened a decade earlier. That's when the Spirit spoke to Jeff's heart after J.D. Hill, former all-pro receiver for the Buffalo Bills, preached at Light of Christ. An avid sports fan, Jeff attended the service only because he wanted to hear more about J.D.'s exploits as an athlete. When J.D. told of how he had lost all of his money because of addictions to drugs and alcohol and then described how the Dream Center had helped save his life, Jeff was not only moved—he heard directly from God.

"You will work with the Dream Center," the Lord said to Jeff's spirit.

That afternoon, Jeff told his wife, Gwen, what had happened during the service, and he asked her if he should do what he was directed. "Would you think I was crazy?" he asked.

"Not at all," she responded. "You should do it."

Jeff called me the next day. "I know I'm supposed to do something," he said. "I'm not sure yet what it is." After a few more minutes, he said his first thought was to do a clothing drive for the Dream Center. I told him to give it a try and "let's see where it goes."

There was only one problem. Jeff was utterly terrified to speak in front of other people. The first time he spoke about the drive from the pulpit, his adolescent daughter stood beside him to hold his trembling hand and offer moral support. It's funny; one-on-one, Jeff is as outgoing and easy to talk to as they come, but public speaking is a whole different story. Though he stammered, Jeff plodded through the difficulty with determined obedience to do what God had asked him to do.

That first year, Jeff and the team of volunteers he assembled from the church delivered twenty-two bags and boxes of clothing to the Dream Center. The next year the donation increased to thirty-seven bags and boxes. As Jeff and the others toured the Dream Center after making the delivery, he noticed one of the men from the church, a person he only knew as an acquaintance, lagging behind the rest of the group. Jeff watched the man looking up and down the Dream Center facility, lost in his own thoughts. *This guy's hooked*, Jeff thought to himself. He approached the man.

"Hey, what's going on?" Jeff asked.

"You know what?" he said. "We can do more."

Jeff later said, "I never asked him, 'Do you want to be a partner in this?' He never asked me, 'Can I be a partner?' It just happened." The man's name was Jeff Ford—and since then, the two Jeff's have coordinated the delivery of nearly five hundred huge bags and boxes of clothing and approximately 16,000 pounds of food to the Dream Center courtesy of Light of Christ. Jeff Ford has also volunteered at our thrift store, Hidden Treasures. We began this store with the focus on using the proceeds to help us build our church building, but God had other, better plans. All proceeds from the thrift store now go to help broken, hurting people. The Lord has so blessed this ministry that there is always a surplus of clothing. Through Jeff's connection to both ministries, the Dream Center sends a truck every two weeks to pick up this surplus and distribute it to people in need.

Jeff and Jeff have also recently started an annual food collection prior to Mother's Day so that the Dream Center can prepare a delicious meal for many of the mothers under their care. Gwen Pfingsten has also been fired and inspired by the Holy Spirit into a ministry all of her own. She now runs an annual backpack drive for children in need. Almost 160 backpacks have been collected in the last two years. The Dream Center servants distribute them to the precious children. Praise be to God!

All of this began when one ordinary man heard from his extraordinary Lord and decided to obey. Now that the Lord has brought the two Jeffs together, nothing will stop them! One Sunday morning, I asked them to stand up during the service. "How much arm twisting did I do to get you to do this?" One answered, "Not too much." Everyone laughed. I then asked, "Will you ever stop this ministry?" They both shook their heads. "Never," Jeff Ford said. "Why?" I asked. Both thought for a moment, and then Jeff Pfingsten responded, "It is our job."

⁜

The individual ministries the Lord puts on your heart is not as important as learning a Spirit-led process. That is really the point of this book: learning a process that the Lord will bless in any congregation, any ministry, and any person; to allow the Holy Spirit full access to do with us whatever He desires. The Lord doesn't want cookie-cutter churches, ministries, pastors or people. This is not a program. It is a process. There is absolutely no way to shortcut this process. He wants us to become who we are meant to be, and *becoming* is difficult! But it is worth every ounce of faith, hope, and love. It is hard work as we trust and allow the Holy Spirit to refine us day by day. There is no way to speed it along. Discipleship was very difficult in Jesus' day—and nothing has changed.

This taught me something I had never realized and, my sense is, many pastors still don't understand. If we, as a ministry, simply seek Jesus and then ask Him how He wants us to serve others, He will be the One to ignite people's hearts to action! Allow people a vision of servant ministry and the Spirit will get to work. He will heal their past hurts. He will help them overcome their fears. We don't need to do any of that as their pastor. The Holy Spirit will take care of it all.

Every Tuesday, the Dream Center offers a one-hour tour, and I facilitated getting many of the members of Light of Christ to take these weekly tours. The idea was simple: if I could expose more people to what God was doing at the Dream Center, they would catch that Holy Spirit servant fire. Every time we had the joy of going to the Dream Center for a tour, we were introduced to incredible people, each with a miraculous story of God's wondrous ways.

Jim is a shining example. He calls himself "One-arm Jim" as a reminder of where he has been. Jim has one arm because heroin use destroyed the other.

Jim lived in South Mountain, a dominate feature in the Valley of the Sun. It rises out of the desert from what used to be south of Phoenix. Now the metropolis surrounds the mountain, so it's not really "south" mountain anymore. However, calling it simply "mountain" is silly, so South Mountain remains. But I digress. There are parks and hiking trails. Tons of radio and cell phone towers are on top of South Mountain, and there is also a beautiful drive that takes visitors to a majestic overview of the entire city. The mountain is alive with activity most every day. Unknown to many, though, is that South Mountain also has caves—so when I say Jim lived *in* South Mountain, it is because he lived in one of those caves.

As he reached out to love and serve others, the Lord brought healing to Jim. The Holy Spirit gave this dear brother in Christ a more beautiful life than he had ever known.

Jim was our tour guide on a visit to the Dream Center. He told us how he used to survive in his cave. He'd come down from the mountain, buy some heroin from his dealer, and sell some of it to make more money. He then bought some groceries and, with the rest of the heroin, climb back up to his "home." He stayed in the cave until both the groceries and the heroin ran out. Sometimes this took a few weeks. Then he'd come back down the mountain for more heroin and groceries. He said his appearance frightened most people. Many assumed he had lost his mind. At that point in his life, he said, they were probably right.

One day as he left his cave, Jim began crying out to Jesus. He knew that if something drastic didn't happen in very short order, he'd end up dead. He also knew he was helpless to overcome his addiction, so he called out to the Lord. "Lord, you must do something! You have to save me from this life because I can't do it myself. Please, Lord. Please!"

He said that the moment his shoes hit the street that day, he was surrounded by four police cars. The officers arrested him, handcuffed him, and put him in the back of a police cruiser—though they had rather confused looks on their faces. He said it was probably because he was shouting, "Thank you, Jesus! I love you, Jesus! I praise you, Lord!" the entire time, and doubted they ever had the privilege before of taking such a joyful person into custody.

Jim spent a few months in prison, sobered up, and was given the option of early release if he agreed to voluntarily go to the Dream Center. By then, his relationship with Jesus was growing and he was excited to be part of the discipleship ministry at the Dream Center. At this glorious place of Holy Spirit miracles, the Lord began transforming Jim's life. He read the Bible like never before. He began exercising and eating healthy meals, practicing more discipline in his life. And he began serving. The Dream Center has over 110 outreaches to broken, hurting people and feeds over 12,000 people every week. As he reached out to love and serve others, the Lord brought healing to Jim.

The Holy Spirit gave this dear brother in Christ a more beautiful life than he had ever known. He restored his physical health, even though he lost an arm to heroin use. The Lord regenerated Jim's mind because it had become, as he put it, a chaotic and horrifyingly confused place. The Lord even restored his relationships. The third time I saw Jim he could hardly contain himself. He was going to get to see his daughter for the first time in twenty years! She had even purchased a plane ticket for him to visit her. He was going to get to see his grandchildren for the first time. Praise be to God!

Jim shared the secret to succeeding at the Dream Center and catching hold of the new life, the dream, the Holy Spirit has for you: "Submission, pure and simple. If you are not willing to completely submit your life to Jesus, learn to listen to Him, and obey Him, nothing will change." That's no different for any of us.

Jesus proclaimed, "I tell you, among those born of women none is greater than John." (Luke 7: 28) John the Baptist was a great, powerful man of God because he was also an incredibly humble, Spirit-filled man of God. "I baptize you with water for repentance, but he who is coming after me is mightier than I, whose sandals I am not worthy to carry. He will baptize you with the Holy Spirit and fire." (Matthew 3: 11) He knew his place in God's plan. He also knew who the actual Savior was: 'The next day he saw Jesus coming toward him, and said, "Behold, the Lamb of God, who takes away the sin of the world!"' And his words "He must increase, but I must decrease." (John 3:30) are a wonderful prayer for us today: *Lord Jesus, get me out of my own way. Fill me with your Holy Spirit and lead the way. You must increase in me, so I must decrease. Make my life less about me and more about you. I want to live for you today. Please show me how to do that. I love you. In your name I pray, Amen*

I became a regular at the Dream Center and met miraculous brothers and sisters in Christ who had come from the most tragic of situations, situations that had humbled them all, but now they shined with the light of the Lord! More than that, each one is like a lighthouse to me, casting a beacon into some of the darkest areas in America. Every person had a miraculous story of God's grace, provision, and new life. I saw a peace, joy, and love in their eyes that few seem to have in the nine-to-five world. They also gave all the of the glory and praise to God our Father for saving them, redeeming them, and renewing them—while also thanking all of their brothers and sisters at the Dream Center who encouraged and believed in them.

Through facilitating the Dream Center tours, I simply showed the members of my church the precious people, the transforming work of the Holy Spirit, and the *need*. I didn't have to preach a sermon series or install a new program. I got people there so they could *see* what God was doing, and the Spirit moved upon their hearts to help others. All I did was watch and pray as people at Light of Christ grew in Jesus and in their joy of the Lord—a genuine, Holy Spirit blessed joy that came only from listening and obeying our living God. As the Holy Spirit led and broke our hearts for our fellow brothers and sisters, people used their gifts to serve and love others, and our Father rewarded our obedience with joy and power!

This laser focus on Jesus, humbling ourselves, and leading by example is lifted up in the following words from our Lord:

"But you are not to be called rabbi, for you have one teacher, and you are all brothers. And call no man your father on earth, for you have one Father, who is in heaven. Neither be called instructors, for you have one instructor, the Christ. The greatest among you shall be your servant. Whoever exalts himself will be humbled, and whoever humbles himself will be exalted. But woe to you, scribes and Pharisees, hypocrites! For you shut the kingdom of heaven in people's faces. For you neither enter yourselves nor allow those who would enter to go in." (Matthew 23:8-13)

Prayerfully consider these words from Frederick Beuchner: "The place God calls us to is the place where your deep gladness and the world's deep hunger meet."

Who is that for you? Where is that for you? Who can you love and serve without needing anything, not even a "thank you," in return? Break out of the business of religion and into the adventure Jesus has for you! As you point everyone to Him, they actually begin to look to Him. As you humble yourself, the Spirit gives people a vision of what life can be. As you joyfully pour yourself out to others, the Holy Spirit inspires that desire in others. No matter what, get hungry for this life. Jesus died to give you the freedom to live it! Desire this life as much as Jesus desires it for you. "For freedom Christ has set us free; stand firm therefore, and do not submit again to a yoke of slavery." (Galatians 5:1) The Holy Spirit will power this new life in Christ, you will shine your light, and God will get all the glory.

Katie Davis Majors is a hero of mine. At eighteen, she traveled to Uganda and found her heart waiting for her. After graduating high school, she moved there to begin caring for the beautiful people in that country. In a very short time she began adopting children. Her book, *Kisses from Katie*, is an incredible read which I highly recommend. Just be sure to have a big box of tissues handy.

Once, during a trip back in America, Katie was talking with her daughter Christine in Uganda. Christine pleaded with "Mommy" for her five-year-old cousin, Joyce, to come and be part of their growing family as well. (The family topped out at thirteen girls!) Katie joyfully agreed. She spoke with Joyce on the phone. "At that point Joyce knew me only as a strange voice. She had no idea who 'Mommy' was and why the others were so excited about me. I longed to take her into my arms and explain to her that I would be there soon and that I would love and care for her forever. I longed to speak love and tenderness over the darkest corners of her young life. But what struck me most about that first phone call with Joyce was what she said to me: 'Thank you for food, Mommy. Today I am still alive.' My heart stopped. This little girl, at five years old, is simply thankful to have something to eat so she can stay alive."

How can I be a worship leader if I am not worshipping?
And what happens to a person's spiritual life if they
never truly praise and worship God from their heart?

There is a power at work on all of us in America. It is the illusion of self-sufficiency, and it impacts every one of us. It is part of our environment. To me, it is like visiting a well-stocked buffet. I don't feel the need to taste everything that is offered, but I definitely eat more than my fill. After all that consumption, all I want to do is sleep for a few days. The same thing happens in our spiritual lives. We are created to receive God's immense love and then pour it out to broken, hurting people! When we focus instead on being served, building *our* ministries, paying the bills, making the maximum yearly contribution to our IRAs, and creating a name for ourselves, our spirits fall asleep. Break my heart for others and wake me up, Lord!

This even happened to Katie. It actually took her a couple of days to get the fire back when she returned to Uganda from the United States. "The second morning, Agnes looked at me and said, 'There it is! It came back!' I asked her groggily, 'What came back?' With joy she could hardly contain, she replied, 'That light that lives in your eyes!'"

Is that light living in your eyes? If not, don't beat yourself up about it. It is astonishingly easy for our spirits to fall asleep in America. Don't worry. Jesus is here. There is no condemnation in Him. He has not given up on us. He has not given up on you! Get up early, seek His kingdom and

His righteousness, follow Him as He loves hurting people through you, and He will ignite that light that lives in your eyes.

Day by day, moment by moment, God opposed my ego, stamping it down as I, in humility, watched Him work in the lives of the people. As this happened, a completely unexpected and awesome change began to occur. Worship on Sunday mornings became less about the order of service and making sure we ended on time, and more about letting the Spirit move in our midst and do what He wanted, for as long as He wanted. The Lord transitioned our worship at Light of Christ from performance to simply an expression of love to our Lord. He loves us back even more!

Up to that point I'm not sure if I ever truly worshipped our Father while I was leading worship. It begs the question: How can I be a worship leader if I am not worshipping? And what happens to a person's spiritual life if they *never* truly praise and worship God from their heart? What if that person is a ministry leader? What if that person is the *pastor*? I had inadvertently slipped into acting like I was worshipping. Jesus speaks to this as well as He quotes Isaiah. "This people honors me with their lips, but their heart is far from me." (Matthew 15: 8) Our Father wants our hearts in worship. The more we love Him, the more we will praise Him, "Because your steadfast love is better than life, my lips will praise you." (Psalm 63:3)

The Lord convicted my heart, mind and soul; don't waste Sunday morning worship by trying to control it. Instead, prepare as the Lord directs and then let the Spirit do whatever He wants in the service. As a pastor, I learned that I was there to worship God just like everybody else. It was liberating both for me and for Light of Christ. I remember speaking to a men's Bible discussion group one day after the previous Sunday's worship had gone longer than scheduled. "When the Spirit's there," one of them said, "you don't care how long the worship is. It's when the Spirit is not there that you start watching the clock."

I am convinced that two of Satan's greatest temptations to ministry leaders are, 1) to never truly worship God on Sunday mornings, and 2) to neglect any time to study and meditate on His Word for my own personal discipleship. The liar and accuser whispers to us as ministry leaders, "*You can do it on your own.*" No, we can't! We can't do anything without God. Jesus said so! Even more, we are to ruthlessly seek to *abide* in Christ as He teaches in John 15.

> "I am the true vine, and my Father is the vinedresser. Every branch in me that does not bear fruit he takes away, and every branch that does bear fruit he prunes, that it may bear more fruit. Already you are clean because of the word that I have spoken to you. Abide in me, and I in you. As the branch cannot bear fruit by itself, unless it abides in the vine, neither can you, unless you abide in me. I am the vine; you are the branches. Whoever abides in me and I in him, he it is that bears much fruit, for apart from me you can do nothing. If anyone does not abide in me he is thrown away like a branch and withers; and the branches are gathered, thrown into the fire, and burned. If you abide in me, and my words abide in you, ask whatever you wish, and it will be done for you. By this my Father is glorified, that you bear much fruit and so prove to be my disciples." (John 15:1-8)

Jesus is the vine, we are the branches, and our Father is the Vinedresser. Yet even as we abide in Him, pruning is always required. If I'm not producing fruit (defined as evidence of my relationship with God that results in service to others to His glory), my branch will be cut off. But here's the thing. Even when I *am* producing fruit, I will still be pruned so that I can produce more and better fruit for Him. In humility, I also needed to understand that everything our Father prunes is something I thought I needed or I would have already removed it myself! If I started with the Spirit, am I now trying to do this by human effort? Prune it, Father! Is ministry becoming more about me than about Him? Prune it, Father! Am I competing against anyone? Prune it, Father!

The astonishing point is this: the pruning process never ends. Get used to it. Do not shortcut the process. The Vinedresser loves us and knows what He is doing. As we humbly and hungrily allow the Spirit to continually change us, knowing that what He prunes is actually *good* for us, the Lord will use our example to give others permission to do the same.

That's exactly what happened next. There was another ego-driven aspect to my character that was about to be chopped away. I never saw it coming. I was even upset and felt like quitting for a while. But now I cannot praise the Lord enough for surrounding me with such faithful brothers and sisters in Christ who allowed me to become the leader I believe I was always meant to be. More than that, I believe this allowed me to start becoming the man of God I was always meant to be.

Chapter 4

---

*Humble yourselves, therefore, under the mighty hand of
God so that at the proper time he may exalt you, casting all
your anxieties on him, because he cares for you.*

1 Peter 5:6-7

Like most pastors, I originally saw my job as one in which I prepared sermons, planned powerful worship experiences, scheduled announcements that needed to be made, organized and orchestrated all special events, grew the ministry, and made sure the income exceeded the expenses. Those were just the basic tasks. I also selected and met weekly with those overseeing all of our other ministries: our preschool, children's and youth groups, men's and women's Bible study groups, and our outreach, evangelism, and finance efforts.

In short, I was responsible for everything. Everyone reported to me. As ministry leader, I was the end-all for everything we did in the ministry. I believe that was the way it was supposed to be—and I micromanaged it all to the core.

I have never met anyone who enjoys being micromanaged, except those who have lost all self-confidence and simply want to be told what to do. I even thought I liked micromanaging, not realizing it was motivated by fear. As micromanager, it was my role to keep Pastor Moe's mighty ministry machine running smoothly, and if someone tried to take a ministry in a different direction, it was also my task to get them back on track. I was diplomatic as possible, of course, but that didn't keep me from gently showing them the error of their ways. After all, I am the shepherd, and the shepherd knows what direction to go. Certainly God hasn't given that information to the sheep! Right?

Yet even as the Holy Spirit was working in my life to give the church back to the Lord, and as He was moving in the lives of the sheep, the wonderful people at Light of Christ, to make us a more servant-focused ministry, my micromanagement mode of operation led to a situation that made it clear it was time for the micromanager in me to be cut off from the vine. The Holy Spirit wanted to take His rightful place as Micromanager in my life and in His church—and it culminated in a decisive meeting with the church board in 2004.

I also needed to trust that the Lord was at work
in all of our hearts, not just mine. The beautiful people
on the board had heard from God and had gently
but firmly changed fifty percent of my job in one night!

I could've seen it coming. Just days before the meeting, board president Dave Ihlenfeld stopped by my office and leaned against the frame of my open door. We engaged in some small talk as we usually do, and then he shared a thought about the staff structure of the church.

"You know, it's really good to keep things centralized," he said casually. "Instead of having a bunch of committees and meetings, we could have a ministry that runs all of the children's stuff, another for the youth, and so on. That could really free you up for more prayer and things like that."

I looked at him, unsure of what to say—because I wasn't really clear on what he was saying in the first place. His expression suggested he knew I didn't understand. But he let it go, and so did I.

The night of the board meeting, Dave and fellow board member Jackie Cooper lovingly and sensitively laid out their idea. They proceeded to list all of the ministries within the church and asked who was responsible to oversee each one. "I am," I answered over and over, and then concluded, "There is a specific person in charge of each one, and they report directly to me."

"Moe," Dave said, "we want you to be *only* our spiritual leader."

I was taken aback. "That's what I'm doing."

"No," he said. "Under this structure, the board will oversee all of those ministries. The ministry coordinators will be responsible to the board from the standpoint of budget needs, staffing, and so on. From a spiritual standpoint, then, everyone will be accountable to you, the pastor. You'll have the overarching word on spiritual matters. We want you to be only our spiritual leader, and let the ministry leaders handle their responsibilities and, as needed, report to the board."

I respectfully heard what was being said, but I clearly lacked comprehension. I thought for a moment. "So, I want to be clear. Are you telling me you don't want me to go to all of the meetings of every ministry?

"Exactly," he said. "We want you to attend one board meeting each month, and one staff meeting each month, and meet with individual ministry leaders as necessary about their spiritual well-being. We want you to be only our spiritual leader."

In all of my years as a pastor—and in all of my conversations with other pastors—I had never heard of a church board doing this. It has also been my experience that most ministry boards are interested in what the ministry leader *isn't* doing; if anything, they want the ministry leader to do *more*. But now? I was literally dumbfounded.

"If I'm not doing all of these other things, then what am I doing?" I asked. "I don't even know what you are talking about."

I'll never forget Dave's response on behalf of the board.

"Neither do we. Go and find out."

While a part of me was more than a little afraid that the board was simply yanking power away from me so *they* could micromanage me, the larger part of me that had been learning to trust God sensed that He was doing a new work in me and that I needed to start by seeking Him more. I also needed to trust that the Lord was at work in all of our hearts, not just mine. The beautiful people on the board had heard from God and had gently but firmly changed fifty percent of my job in one night!

The ramifications of this structural change cannot be overstated. I believe with all of my heart that the Lord would never have unleashed the miracles we have experienced at Light of Christ if this change had not occurred. He could not have used us as He has if this change had not occurred. Make no mistake: if we do not allow the Holy Spirit to restructure our lives and ministries in such a way that the structure supports and encourages on-going Spirit-led ministry, discipleship will not be allowed to thrive and become part of our spiritual DNA. It will only be a temporary change, and only a matter of time before fear takes over and Micromanaging Moe shows up again in all of his controlling ugliness! The structure either supports or inhibits on-going, Spirit-led transformation.

I believe this structure will be blessed by the Holy Spirit in any Christian ministry, not just churches. There are no sins unique to us. We all deal with the same basic sins of ego, control issues, fear, insecurity, and self-centeredness. Releasing the ministry to the Holy Spirit is essential. We must pray for each other and help one another to do this.

However, what also cannot be overstated is the difficulty for a ministry leader to *allow* this change to take place. For example, if you believe the Lord is ready to create an incredible revival in your congregation by setting your pastor free to become the child of God he was always meant to be, and thereby leading the congregation by example, then I believe those most ready for this change are, in order, 1) the Holy Spirit, 2) the pastor's family, 3) everyone else in the ministry, and 4) the pastor.

Why is it highly likely the pastor will be the most resistant to change, even if your pastor is miserable? Because chances are very good your pastor is afraid just like I was afraid! A ministry leader will generally resist this change tooth and nail, not realizing that an incredible life of freedom, love, miracles, and joyful self-sacrifice is on the other side of releasing control. The *real* person, the life God created him or her to live, is also waiting on the other side. I firmly believe the life I wanted desperately would never have become a reality without God using others to help me get there. That's why it's vital that the Holy Spirit must speak *to* others first, and then He will speak the truth in love *through* them to the ministry leader. As the Holy Spirit convicts other leaders, they will then gently but firmly help the primary ministry leader make this transition. That is what happened at Light of Christ.

I later learned that the structure they put in place originated in part from the business strategy experience Dave and Jackie brought to the table—specific giftings that God had given them. They also said the Holy Spirit had been moving them in that direction without them even knowing at the time what He was doing in the life of the church, and especially in my heart. Dave was inspired by his own personal Bible study of Titus chapters 1-2 and 1 Timothy chapters 3-5 and what they revealed about the operation of the early Christian church and responsibilities of early church leaders. He said it didn't matter to him how other churches did things; he was convicted that the pastor should be free to be in Bible studies with people, praying for people, and serving others, not stuck in meetings and trying to solve every problem. Jackie added that because she had not been brought up in a church setting and didn't even attend a church service until she was twenty-nine years of age, she had no preconceived notions of what a pastor was supposed to do and never had any unreasonable expectations of others in leadership. She simply thought the structure they introduced to me that night made good common sense.

I had thought that effort was the key to everything. Work harder, do more things, get people involved, keep them encouraged, and get them to do what I wanted them to do. If the ministry grows, I will get the credit. If it does not, it might be time to find another ministry! Even though we were doing many good things, we had missed the only essential thing. *I* had missed the only necessary thing! It is even more important than serving others. Jesus tells us what it is:

"Now as they went on their way, Jesus entered a village. And a woman named Martha welcomed him into her house. And she had a sister called Mary, who sat at the Lord's feet and listened to his teaching. But Martha was distracted with much serving. And she went up to him and said, 'Lord, do you not care that my sister has left me to serve alone? Tell her then to help me.' But the Lord answered her, 'Martha, Martha, you are anxious and troubled about many things, but one thing is necessary. Mary has chosen the good portion, which will not be taken away from her.'" (Luke 10:38-42)

Did you see that? Jesus told Martha that Mary was doing the "one" necessary thing. Martha was doing a lot of good things, but missed the singularly necessary thing: listening to Jesus. Who was the angry one; Mary or Martha? Who was judging the other? Who became so frustrated she not only judged Jesus ("don't you care") but she also told Him what He should do! Sound familiar? Who is the one on the road to burnout? I know, because I have done all of those things. Still do. It is a daily struggle for me. We can all get distracted with much serving. Listening to Jesus calms the soul. It is the only necessary thing.

The challenge for me was (and is) that I am not a natural born listener. I am a natural born talker! Occasionally I will listen. However, sometimes it will simply *appear* like I am listening when in reality I am busy thinking about the next thing I want to say, wondering when the talking person will stop talking! Actually listening to others is a *very* difficult thing to do, and if listening is hard in our relationships with family, friends and co-workers, how much more difficult is it with our Heavenly Father? I used to believe Mary was doing nothing in this passage. Now I realize she was doing the single most challenging thing of all: quieting down to listen to Jesus. It is the *only* necessary thing. Don't take my word for it. Jesus says so.

If I am listening to Jesus, He is going to tell me about our Father's perfect and unconditional love for me. If I truly listen, I will be filled with so much of His love that I won't need any more from anyone. I will not use anyone for my ego needs! I will *love* them more but *need* them less. I will just want to pour His love *out*. If I am listening to Jesus, He will remind me that there is a Savior, and I'm not Him! If I am listening to Jesus, He will remind me the ministry belongs to Him and so does the burden. If I am listening to Jesus, He reminds me that He has a good, pleasing, and perfect plan for me, and He is the Way, Truth and Life of that plan. If I am listening to Jesus, He will remind me that He never runs anywhere, so if I want to follow Him I probably need to slow down. If I am listening to Jesus, and He knows what I need to hear, He will give me His peace, encouragement, consolation, forgiveness, conviction, and even a kick to the backside precisely when I need it! He knows. Am I listening? Truly?

✥

Jesus through the power of the Holy Spirit will guide us all day long, showing us where to serve and how to serve. He will bless and empower our work, causing it to be almost effortless because we are drawing our strength and sustenance from Him, not ourselves. His yoke is easy and His burden is light. When we try to do things our way by our power, we will be overwhelmed. Spiritual leaders in ministries must listen to Jesus. He calms us down, powers us up, and leads us into the world. He uses our example to lead others.

> If you are a ministry leader, your primary job is to stay in God's Word, listening to Jesus, and rededicate your life and ministry to the Lord every day.

One of my favorite family photographs is from a Sunday morning where our son, Wade, had repositioned a chair right behind the podium. He then climbed up on it, grabbed hold of the podium, and looked like he was set to preach! He was probably four years old at the time. I remember thinking, "I wonder if Wade has the gifts to be a pastor, because he sure looks the part!"

I believe the structure introduced by our church board fits *any* ministry leader, regardless of one's unique gifting. All people, including pastors, have just a few gifts, so the best thing to do is to listen to Jesus. He will help you understand what your part is and promises to bring gifted people alongside for all of the *other* areas of ministry. They will report to the board and you will encourage them in their walk with Jesus.

If you are a ministry leader, your primary job is to stay in God's Word, listening to Jesus, and rededicate your life and ministry to the Lord every day. You lead others by example. The Holy Spirit will show the leadership team how to restructure the ministry so everyone at every level learns to listen to Jesus. We learn to refocus on using our particular gifts to care for hurting people. The Spirit will do the rest, including raising up people to fill in all of the other ministry areas. As He does, encourage them in those areas and release them to follow Jesus.

Remember, you are to touch base with the leaders, but with no micromanaging. Even Jesus sent His disciples out without looking over their shoulders.

So many ministries are looking for a leader who is a good administrator. It is probably because their structure looks something like this, using a congregational model as an example:

Diagram #1

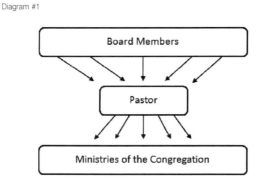

It also produces a rather interesting job for those on the board.

Relaxing at a wedding reception, a gentleman approached me. He told me that he appreciated the wedding service over which I had just presided, and then volunteered, "I am a deacon at my church." Unfamiliar with their organizational structure, I asked him what his responsibilities are. "To watch you!" A cold chill went through my body, and I remember thinking, "And who is watching you?"

A revealing exercise to try in your own ministry is to have everyone draw the structure of your organization. Don't give too much instruction on the front end. It is a wonderful insight to get from your leaders. I believe the most important part of any ministry's organizational structure is where God shows up on the drawing. Sometimes He is nowhere to be found!

Thank you, Lord, for our structure at Light of Christ! This is what it looks like:

Diagram #2

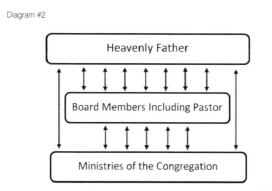

The primary responsibility of each board member is prayer. Since our Father already knows what we need, most of our time communicating with Him is spent *listening*! How can we possibly know what our Father wants to do with His church if we don't ask Him and then learn to listen? Each board member is also a liaison to a ministry team, including the pastor.

As an aside, speaking to congregational leaders, I believe the pastor should oversee worship and music, since worship is a huge part of any pastor's responsibilities. No one should be praying over the worship service more than the pastor, and he should constantly ask, "What do you want this worship service to look like, Heavenly Father? Speak to me. I am listening." I work with our music leader, but the final call is mine. This avoids a great deal of conflict; there's no politicking or arguing. If someone feels something needs to be changed in the worship service, I first ask them to pray about it. Once they have spent significant time in prayer, if they still believe their idea might be of God, I invite them to share it with me. I then seek the Lord's will through prayer and patience. If the Lord confirms the change, we then implement it as the Spirit leads. It's all about prayer and patience, prayer and patience, prayer and patience, and then obedience.

As spiritual leader of the ministries, I also pray for and check in with every ministry coordinator to see how his or her walk with our Father is going. Mostly, I encourage these beautiful brothers and sisters in Christ. It is astonishing what God can do in people's lives if we allow Him to pour love and encouragement through us to them. We turn around (repent), rededicate our lives and ministries to the Lord every day, restructure every ministry to learn to listen to Jesus, refocus on caring for hurting people, and then get ready to rejoice!

Every team is also structured the same way—prayer first, with each member having certain responsibilities within the ministry area. From time to time the board may need to give direction to a particular team. However, if the team members are learning to listen to Jesus, work together, and serve others, very little direction is needed from the board.

I pray you are beginning to see how burnout is next to impossible in Spirit-led ministries! Everything is done through God's power and in His time. How *can* we burn out? At Light of Christ, none of our ministry leaders have experienced burnout with this structure and focus. A very simple phrase I learned from Andy Stanley, pastor of Northpoint Community Church, has helped slow me down. His emphasis upon *sustainable pace* has made a huge difference in my life, and has now become one of our favorite phrases at Light of Christ. Remember, Jesus never hurried anywhere. He not only gives us His amazing grace, but also His amazing pace. I continually remind our leaders to give the ministry back to God. "It belongs to Him," I say. "Let's thank Him for allowing us a very small part in what He is doing." Occasionally, a leader may feel it is time to step down from a ministry area, but the vast majority remain in the church and serve in a different capacity. We have never had to fire anyone. Praise the Lord!

As I set out to "go and find out" what God wanted me to do in my new role as the church's spiritual leader, I recalled how Pastor Barnett once shared that every morning he got up early to spend two hours with the Lord because, as he put it, "there is a lot of Egypt that needs to be marched out of me every day." I resonated with that feeling, so I began prioritizing my own time with God every morning. I disciplined myself to read, be quiet, and listen to what the Lord might be saying to me. I read a chapter of Proverbs a day; those thirty-one chapters line up nicely with the days in a month. But I spent most of my time reading Jesus' words in Matthew, Mark, Luke, and John. I discovered something remarkable about how Jesus spent His time—a plain but vital truth of Scripture that I had apparently missed until now. Each of the four Gospels told how Jesus got up early in the morning to pray and be alone with His Father. This was a priority to Him. How much more so, then, did time alone with our Father need to be my priority.

I once heard of an overseas missionary who was so mindful of his walk with the Lord that he got in the habit of asking the same question of God every thirty seconds or so, "Lord, am I pleasing you now?" Each morning and throughout the day I asked the Lord to, "Please get me out of my own way, fill me with your Spirit, and lead me to empty vessels."

Jamie Fry was one of those vessels the Lord led me to as I went door-to-door—though I didn't know it at first because he didn't respond to my knock. He explained that he was diapering one of his three children while his wife was napping with the others when I came to his home. But I left a pamphlet that invited them to our services, and they decided to stop in one Sunday morning a week or so later. "We met other families who were our age and in our situation with little kids running around, and it felt like a great place to be because it was all about the Bible and what God's looking for us to do," he said. "It wasn't about what this organization called 'church' is expecting us to do, and a lot of the things Pastor Moe was talking about were really salient to us at the time. It was like the kind of things we'd talk about at breakfast or dinner."

Jamie and his wife began serving right away working with kids and helping with our Vacation Bible School. They remained active for a couple of years until they needed to move back east. "We thought, 'Wow, it'll be nice to go to a church where we can just go to church and not have to serve, but just attend,'" Jamie said. "Yet we quickly found we had forgot what it was like to be in a Spirit-led church, one that pulled us in—and once you get in that centrifuge of His love and then be whipped out again in service, there is nothing like it."

In many ways, every ministry
can become a "Dream Center" as
the Lord gives His children the
servant dreams He has for each of us.

A few years later, Jamie's family was able to return to Arizona and found out from a friend that Light of Christ was still meeting, but at a different location. "And it hadn't changed," he said, "but had the same core of energy and people and Spirit. I feel the church should not be an edifice. The church is the people that are doing things."

And has Jamie ever taken "doing things" to heart! He is now serving the Lord and others in awesome ways. He helps out with the church's youth ministry, leads our youth band, and plays guitar and preaches at one of our weekly nursing home outreach services. It is an absolute joy when my schedule allows me to attend that worship service. The Holy Spirit shows up in such immense ways as the love of God fills the room with songs of praise, prayers of compassion and love, and even residents providing important parts of the service. Mary, for example, is a resident at the care facility. It is very difficult for her to read, and yet every week she practices a particular scripture that God puts on her heart so she can share it aloud as part of the worship service. We all look forward to what Mary reads from God's Word. It is so very sweet. Thank you, Lord Jesus, for Mary and her love for you!

Jamie's story is yet another reminder that the ministry belongs to the Lord, so all He needs me to be is a faithful follower whose priority is listening to Him. He will use my example to encourage others. Once they begin discovering the ministries our Lord has for them, watch out! A little bit of encouragement from me is all the Spirit needs to help my brothers and sisters catch fire for Him—then I simply get out of their way. In many ways, every ministry can become a "Dream Center" as the Lord gives His children the servant dreams He has for each of us.

God also helped me to see that every person in the ministry was unique; each one had his or her own story. I also knew the Lord had a beautiful plan for each one, though I had no idea what it was. It's as though He was saying to me, "Moe, if you're Spirit-led and interact with others with no other agenda than to listen to them and care for them, just watch what I'll do. I will heal their hurt, and then heal them even more as I gently lead them out of themselves to care for others!"

That pivotal board meeting was in April. In our last meeting of the year in December, Dave proclaimed the glad news. "Moe, you've never done a better job." They have continued to encourage me to listen to Jesus, follow Him, and serve others ever since.

My spirit rejoiced! I had spent significant time those eight months walking through neighborhoods and simply praying for the families who lived there. I made more hospital visits, meeting with total strangers and offering my prayers and encouragement. I told the church from the pulpit, "A hospital room is the most honest room you'll ever find. Everything is stripped away." I exhorted the people of Light of Christ to seek opportunities to help hurting, broken people. The Spirit helped me learn to quiet my mind, listen, and truly love people where they were. I simply cared for them with the love the Spirit poured into me and through me. I didn't micromanage anything or anyone, nor did I have any desire to. It was liberating!

Consider this: What gets a group of 250-pound super athletes to humble themselves, take a knee, join hands, and pray for the smallest, least athletic guy on the team? When that least athletic guy is about to kick a field goal to win the football game, that's what! And why are they doing such an odd thing? Because they are *passionate* about the outcome of the game.

I have this written on my daily calendar: "If I'm not praying about it I'm not passionate about it." What is more important than to spend time in prayer, bringing people to our Heavenly Father in loving intercession? I began by praying for those in my family. The Lord increased my love for them through the prayers. I then began praying for everyone in our congregation by name a few times each week. The Lord increased my love and passion for them. I began praying for all our brothers and sisters in the persecuted church. He increased my love for and commitment to them. Lately the Lord has added prayers for the lost, world leaders, and even the persecutors to my list. The Lord has shown me that every time I pray for anyone, He increases my love for everyone! Thank you, Jesus!

I also learned a ministry-altering truth that transformed how I saw myself as a leader—one many Christians (and pastors) may struggle to understand, much less believe. By the grace of God, I was permitted to lay down the staff and lie down in green pastures.

Chapter 5

The Lord is my shepherd; I shall not want.
PSALM 23:1

Jesus is the Shepherd of Light of Christ—not me. I believe this applies to any Christian ministry leader: Jesus is the Shepherd and we are His sheep. He is the leader and we are His Spirit-led followers. Whatever leading we do is primarily by our example. We lead others as we follow Him.

From Psalm 23 to John 21, it's clear that the Lord is the shepherd of the sheep (the Christian church, the Body of Christ), not someone else. When Jesus asked Peter, "Do you love me?" three times in John 21, He does not then say, "Feed *your* sheep, Peter." The sheep are *His*. Always have been and always will be. Yet within most Christian circles, the pastor is the shepherd, with each of us having our own flock.

This is somewhat surprising, because according to the ESV translation there is only one passage that suggests this interpretation: "... shepherd the flock of God that is among you, exercising oversight, not under compulsion, but willingly, as God would have you; not for shameful gain, but eagerly." (1 Peter 5:2) In my heart of hearts, I wish Peter had used a different word—perhaps like guide, encourage, direct or even supervise—instead of *shepherd*, because it is such a powerful, even sacred metaphor in the scriptures.

Once we remove the passages that discuss the shepherds in the fields in Luke 2, all *other* New Testament references to "shepherd" point to one individual: Jesus. We even have an example earlier in the same letter from Peter: "For you were straying like sheep, but have now returned to the

Shepherd and Overseer of your souls." (1 Peter 2:25) The Shepherd in this passage is clearly and only Jesus.

Is it possible we have been using the wrong image to inform our self-image as pastors? Are we called to be more like sheep than shepherds? The scriptural evidence is compelling, and the ramifications change everything. At least they did for me.

One definition of a pastor is "a helper or feeder of the sheep." (International Standard Bible Encyclopedia) Let me ask you a question: Isn't a sheep leading by example as he or she stays close to the Shepherd, also a helper and feeder of other sheep? As we feast on the bread of life, the Lord uses our witness to encourage others to join in the feast as well. As we humbly follow the Good Shepherd, the Spirit helps others do the same. As we learn to quietly listen for the Good Shepherd's voice, we model the only necessary thing Jesus has for all of us. As we care for those who are broken, hurting, and in need, we are following the Good Shepherd who leads us to them. He uses our example to inspire others to follow Him and do the same. And the Good Shepherd, the only True Shepherd, gets all the glory—every last ounce of glory!

But here's another problem for many of us as ministry leaders: If you are like me, you have been *trained* to be more like a shepherd than a sheep. This fit nicely with my desire to micromanage. It also matched up with my desire for people to follow and praise me. But it didn't make it right and the Lord would not bless me with Holy Spirit peace, joy, and power until I repented and submitted. Tons of books have been written on leadership. How many on followership? Consider how the roles are drastically different.

> The heart of love that the Spirit will grow in you
> will transform you and inspire others.

If I am a pastor who is a shepherd as traditionally believed, I am in charge. That is a lot of pressure and it can produce a lot of push back, otherwise known as conflict. I need to know where to take the flock and how to get them *moving*! (Anyone know where I can get a cattle prod?) I need to know where there are green pastures and still waters. I need to know how to restore people's souls. I need to resolve every conflict between the sheep. I need to try and keep my sheep happy. The flock belongs to me and I am responsible to grow this flock. My success rides on my ability to get more and more sheep into the fold, because I think that's what Jesus wants. I must learn more and better techniques to accomplish this. I must be sure we change the worship service, perhaps by taking out any of that "sin" or "cross" or "repentance" or even "Jesus" talk which might upset some people, so they will return next week. I must prioritize going to a shepherding conference once a year so I can commiserate with other shepherds about how difficult our jobs are as well as find out the latest, greatest, newest shepherding techniques. At the end of my life, I will give a report to the Chief Shepherd.

Now let's look at being a pastor who is a sheep. All that I have to do is stay close to the True Shepherd, Jesus! Glancing up from my grazing every thirty seconds or so makes sense so I don't wander too far off. Helping others in the flock stay close or come back to our Shepherd is important as well, as He loves them as much as He loves me. He is crazy about us all! Keeping my ears attentive to the voice of the Shepherd is the only necessary thing to develop so that when He calls, I will follow. "He calls his own sheep by name and leads them out. When he has brought out all his own, he goes before them, and the sheep follow him, for they know his voice." (John 10:3b-4) And again, "The thief comes only to steal and kill and destroy. I came that they may have life and have it abundantly. I am the good shepherd. The good shepherd lays down his life for the sheep." (John 10:10-11)

Jesus the Shepherd calms us down by reminding us of His love, presence, power and provision. Through the leading of the Holy Spirit, the Good Shepherd will gently and patiently guide each of us along paths of self-sacrificial righteousness for His name's sake, which is the life prepared for us to live. Only Jesus knows the specifics of the plans He has for you. However, His call to follow Him implies movement. I heard the analogy that it is difficult to steer a parked car. Get moving. Jesus will steer and direct you through the Holy Spirit. Try different things! Get outside yourself, serve others with absolutely no expectation of reward and see what God will do with that. The heart of love that the Spirit will grow in you will transform you and inspire others.

I recall when my daughter sang a solo during her kindergarten play at school. I was pretty anxious for her because she was going to perform without any musical accompaniment; a five-year-old girl singing a cappella in front of over four hundred students and parents. I did my job videotaping my little princess because we wanted to preserve the moment (I later accidentally taped over her performance with a meaningless football game!) and I was praying for her. She did great. Later, I asked her if she was nervous. To my surprise, she said, "No." When I asked why, she raised her eyebrows and said in a voice way beyond her years, "Daaaaad—Jesus was with me." I probably should have known that, being a pastor and all. What is there to fear? Jesus *is* with us! The Good Shepherd is here.

As we follow Jesus and serve others, one of two things will happen: either people will notice or they will not. It is okay that they notice, with one qualifier: in Matthew 5, Jesus tells us we are the light of the world and to let our lights shine! "In the same way, let your light shine before others, so that they may see your good works and give glory to your Father who is in heaven." (Matthew 5:16) The provision is that our Father gets all of the glory all of the time. And what do we get? Freedom! We are set free from trying to impress anyone. We love others the way He has first loved us, without conditions, and whatever glory comes our way we immediately redirect to Him.

And if no one notices? Really praise God for that! According to our Lord, this is where the greatest personal reward resides, because it comes only from our Heavenly Father:

Beware of practicing your righteousness before other people in order to be seen by them, for then you will have no reward from your Father who is in heaven. Thus, when you give to the needy, sound no trumpet before you, as the hypocrites do in the synagogues and in the streets, that they may be praised by others. Truly, I say to you, they have received their reward. But when you give to the needy, do not let your left hand know what your right hand is doing, so that your giving may be in secret. And your Father who sees in secret will reward you.

And when you pray, you must not be like the hypocrites. For they love to stand and pray in the synagogues and at the street corners, that they may be seen by others. Truly, I say to you, they have received their reward. But when you pray, go into your room and shut the door and pray to your Father who is in secret. And your Father who sees in secret will reward you." (Matthew 6:1-6)

Become the "secret" servant and prayer at home, at work, and in your neighborhood. Our Father notices. You are doing this for Him. No one else needs to know. And since they don't *know*, they can't even *thank you*. It's almost like a detox program as the Lord sets us free from seeking people's praise! Besides, Jesus promises there is an infinitely better reward. It comes from our Father. And what is the reward? He gives you all of the joy, love, and encouragement you will ever need as He whispers, "I am proud of you" into your heart, mind, and soul. It is *pure* power! The world can never give this to you or take it from you.

You will also confuse a lot of people in the process as they ask, "Who in the world is doing all of these nice things?"

In the first year of marriage, a friend of mine spoke with a man who had been married for fifty years. The older gentleman asked him, "Do you know what the perfect percentage is in marriage?"

"Absolutely," responded my friend. "It's fifty-fifty."

"Nope," replied the older man. "It's actually one hundred to zero."

"What?" my newlywed friend asked. "That can't be right. I give fifty percent and she gives fifty percent."

The gentleman smiled. "We always score ourselves better than we should. Belief that marriage is fifty-fifty has caused lots of marriages to break up. No scorecard. The perfect percentage is to give all of yourself and expect nothing in return. It is the expectation that stops us."

What incredible insight! Think about it: isn't that precisely what unconditional love means? This is our Father's love for each of us! The Lord gives all of Himself to me whether I ever give Him back anything at all. Of course, when I begin pouring love back into Him and loving others the way He loves me, I come alive in Holy Spirit power that cannot be stopped. There are no expectations of any reciprocity of love; I pour out to God and to others the unconditional love He has poured into me! As Jesus said, "A new command I give you: Love one another. As I have loved you, so you must love one another." (John 13:34) Allow Christ in you to love others as He has loved you: unconditionally and extravagantly!

We come alive in Holy Spirit power, become a new creation through His new mercies every day, and lead others by example. Remember in the Gospel of Luke how Jesus told His disciples to stay in the city of Jerusalem until they were filled with power from on high? (Luke 24: 49) They weren't ready to be His witnesses until they were Holy Spirit filled. The same thing applies to us. We will discover what it means to be Holy Spirit filled and spilled as we deny ourselves, take up our crosses daily, and follow Jesus to broken, hurting, helpless, and lonely sheep—and we will be healed in the process. Ask our Father to fill you with the Holy Spirit. He wants you to! (Luke 11:13)

Nobody is a nobody to God.
Everybody is a somebody to God.

With each day, we uncover the unique ministries we were created by Him to do. It might be in the nursing homes or prisons. Maybe it's serving as a chaplain at a police station or in a hospital. Maybe the good Shepherd will lead you to a soup kitchen to love and care for those who wonder if they matter to anyone. Maybe it is going to your local elementary school and reading to children. Jesus knows! Listen for the voice of the Shepherd and follow Him.

We recently had a "Dixie Cup Sunday" at Light of Christ. Before the children leave for Sunday school, I always get time with them at the front of the worship area. This time I had them form up in lines like the spokes of a wheel extending out from me. Each line was no more than seven children. Every child then received a Dixie cup. I invited those in the interior of the lines to hold their cups so I could pour water from a massive pitcher into each one. They were then instructed that they could not drink the water, nor did I want them to spill any water on the ground, if possible. However, I wanted to pour *all* of the water from the huge pitcher into their little cups. "How are we going to accomplish that?" I asked. The children thought hard for a few seconds. Then I offered, "What if you turn around and pour your cup of water into the child's cup behind you?" They immediately understood the idea, poured into the child behind them, who in turn did the same. I then poured more into their cups, and they once again poured into the children behind them. Before long, the huge pitcher was almost empty and the Dixie cups were full. The children then drank the delicious water. I then gave them lots of cups, inviting them to pass out one to every family in worship as a reminder that no matter how small the cup, huge amounts of water can pass through it.

The same is true for each of us. Our Heavenly Father wants to pour an almost infinite amount of His soul-satisfying faith, hope and love to us and through us. It only depends upon how many people we're willing to pour into; to love them as He loves us. Worry restricts the love flow. Judging others stops it cold. That's why our job is not to worry or judge. Our job is to receive the perfect love of God and then pour into everyone. The more the merrier.

I read an inspiring book entitled *Jesus Prom* by Jon Weece, who follows the Good Shepherd in Kentucky. I recommend this book to you as an incredible example how the Spirit reveals to followers of Jesus wonderfully creative and unique ways of caring for people. For example, for over a decade of Tuesday mornings Jon has placed himself on downtown street corners, mostly outside the area courthouse, with a sign that reads, "Free Hugs." As part of sentencing, a local judge sends those he convicts out to Jon. One time a man stopped because he thought it read, "Free Hogs." Another time a lady pulled up to him on a bicycle. Unable to read, she asked him what the sign said. He told her.

"Are you for real?" she asked.

"Come a little closer and find out," he responded.

She did and he hugged her. When he tried to pull away, she pulled him in tighter. She buried her head in his chest and said, "Nobody's hugged me in a long time." As he put it, "When nobody hugs you, you begin to feel like a nobody. Nobody is a nobody to God. Everybody is a somebody to God." Jon is following Jesus to broken, hurting people. The Good Shepherd uses his example to encourage others to do the same.

Jesus desires every disciple and ministry to be great, but only by His standards. "Jesus called them to him and said to them, 'You know that those who are considered rulers of the Gentiles lord it over them, and their great ones exercise authority over them. But it shall not be so among you. But whoever would be great among you must be your servant, and whoever would be first among you must be slave of all. For even the Son of Man came not to be served but to serve, and to give his life as a ransom for many.'" (Mark 10:42-45)

The first congregation I had the privilege to serve was located in West Phoenix. It was in a pretty rough area of town. The congregation had decided to put bars on all of the windows. My first impression was, "Are those to keep people out or me in?" Protection or prison? Far too many days I have lived in the prison of fear, insecurity, selfishness, loneliness, and self-loathing. Perhaps it is more than a prison. Perhaps it is a tomb. Remember, Jesus did not go into Lazarus' tomb. He stood on the outside and called Lazarus out! "The dead man came out, his hands and feet wrapped with strips of linen, and a cloth around his face. Jesus said to them, "Take off the grave clothes and let him go."' (John 11: 44 NIV)

One of my favorite prayers is simply, "Lord Jesus, please keep me from dying until I'm dead!"

Listen to the Shepherd. He will lead you out of the tomb of self and into the miraculous life prepared for you. He will surround you with others who will help as well. This life will break your heart to love Him and others like never before. I have no idea what that life is. Neither do you. That's part of the adventure! Only the Shepherd knows. With Him, there are no cookie-cutter ministries and no cookie-cutter children; no short-cutting of the process and no shortcutting of His promise.

He gets all the glory when you allow Him to make you uniquely you.

⁜

As a mission developing pastor, I was required to knock on doors to invite people to the new congregation we were starting. No part of me wanted to do this. Generally speaking, I do not like it when strangers knock on our door at home. However, as I look back now I praise God that I was forced to do this as part of my call. I do not believe I would have had the courage to do so any other way. I encourage you to pray about it, get out of the boat, and give it a try! Every door is a new adventure.

I cannot tell you the number of beautiful encounters I've had walking through neighborhoods, praying for families I do not know, and getting to meet people at their front doors. Many people who are now at Light of Christ decided to visit because of this initial encounter. And the fears I once had? They are still there, but the Lord has given me some pretty freeing insights: 1) No one needs to answer the door if they don't want to; 2) Mailers may be more efficient, but not for breaking and growing my heart for God and the people in our neighborhoods; 3) Every person is immensely interesting, and with Jesus leading the way I am learning to love them before I even meet them; and 4) I am actually not going door-to-door to get them to come to Light of Christ. I am following Jesus door-to-door to let them know how much they are loved by our Heavenly Father. If He brings them to Light of Christ, praise God! If he moves in their hearts to start going back to their former congregation, praise God! If the Lord is using me to plant a seed in someone's heart that won't manifest itself for two decades, praise God! We won't know that until we get to Heaven, and frankly, we don't need to know. We simply need to be obedient and live the adventure the Lord has prepared for us. His reward is all we need.

I always pray as I walk up to a new home. I ask the Lord to give me His love for them and for Him to take over the conversation. On one hot Arizona afternoon, I was spending time with Jesus and knocking on doors of people He loves when a man opened his door. As I broke into my little greeting, a smile came to his face and he asked me, "Would you like some water?"

"That would be great," I responded.

"Well, come on in and rest." The Lord gave me peace about it, so I walked into his home. As we talked, I discovered he was a Christian missionary from Africa who was back in America for a few weeks. I asked him to share some of his stories. It was awesome! Then I questioned, "Is there a difference between Christians in Africa and here in America?" He slowly nodded his head and then said, "Probably the simplest way to describe it is through their prayers. Christians in America ask God to remove their burdens. Christians in Africa ask God for stronger backs." Wow! Thank you, Jesus—and give me a stronger back.

You also meet many people who want absolutely nothing to do with religion. I knocked on one door, stepped back, and a young man opened the door. I said my greeting and he responded, "Yeah, I don't think you'll be seeing us."

"Really? Why is that?"

"We are atheists."

Before I could stop myself (and there was no reason to), I clapped my hands, pointed both index fingers at him, and said, "We love atheists!"

It was so unexpected to both of us that we immediately began to laugh. After a few seconds, I shook my head, wiped away a joyful tear, and said, "But seriously, if you ever do feel God tugging at your heart, please give us a try. We would love to have you join us." He smiled, nodded, and said, "We will."

No pressure at all—just simply loving others as we follow Jesus, shining His light.

You absolutely never know what is going to happen when that door opens. One man told me I was the first Christian who ever knocked on his door. At another home, a young lady opened. I always take a step back to make the person feel more at ease. I said my greeting and she responded, "No, I really don't have anything to do with church anymore."

I looked right at her and words that I had not planned or said before, and have never said since, came out of my mouth.

"What happened to you?"

Her eyes widened and then filled with tears. She began to cry right in front of me. I immediately thought, *Oh man, Redding, what have you gotten yourself into now? Lord, help me.* And she continued to cry. Fifteen seconds. Thirty. Forty-five. She wasn't going back inside, she was incapable of speaking, and the tears were pouring out of her. I felt compelled by the Spirit to reach out to her in brotherly love. I took off my hat, stepped forward, put my hand on her shoulder, and prayed, "Dear Jesus, please help this dear child of yours. Help her to know how much you love her. Heal her heart. Heal this hurt in her. Let her know how precious she is to you. So many have been hurt by people in your church. Please forgive us. Heal us all. Love us all back to life. We love you, Jesus. In your name we pray, Amen."

When Jesus enters our hearts,
minds, and souls, He does not come alone.
He always brings the entire world with Him!

The beautiful child of God mumbled a word of thanks as she stepped back into her home and closed the door. We never saw her at Light of Christ, but she has never left my heart and mind. There are so many broken, hurting people out there. Some have even been hurt by people in congregations. Will we allow the Lord to break our hearts for them? Will we follow Jesus to them? Some people will never come to church, so we must go to them. That's what Jesus did. Plus, it is a great time to spend with the Lord in prayer and praise! Now I am actually singing to the Lord as I travel from door to door. It is wonderful and *never* boring. And as I mentioned, behind every door is one of the neatest people you will ever meet.

When Jesus enters our hearts, minds, and souls, He does not come alone. He always brings the entire world with Him! He gives us a loving burden for every person on the face of the Earth, but a very specific *calling* to reach out to some. You have a calling. Never doubt it. Our Father has specific people for Christ in you to serve, love, and encourage, and the vast majority of them may never know your name. That's okay, because the Good Shepherd knows your name, and He is calling you by name to follow Him to them. When you find those you are called to love and care for, the Lord has another surprise in store for you.

When our twins, Wade and Micah, were very young they loved to play hide-and-seek. We'd be out in the back yard. I'd cover my face and begin counting. They'd scurry off, discussing their strategy in incredibly loud whispers the entire way. Regardless, I knew the general area where I could find them. Their hiding place was behind some bushes around the side of the house. Not only that, when I finished the count and proclaimed, "Ready or not, here I come!" they immediately started calling out, "Here we are, Dad! Over here!" As I rounded the corner of the house, there they were, waving their arms with huge smiles on their faces. I'd laugh and respond, "I found you!" They giggled and nodded. We played this game over and over again. It never got old.

When the Lord knows we are truly searching for *Him*—not for what He can *do* for us—He will be found. He is waving His arms, calling our names, and shouting, "Here I am!" He's hidden, but not really. The Bible tells us where He is. And *we* didn't really find Him. He revealed Himself to us. Jesus tells us when we care for the broken and hurting, when we reach out to those we are created and called to serve, we have also found Him! "You found me! Now, let's care for this precious child of mine together!" Jesus is overjoyed to be found in these priceless people. He breaks our hearts for them and it is very difficult to go back to our old, small, boring, self-centered lives!

The cool thing is the search never gets old. He always has people for us to love. It is *always* the same joy when we find Jesus in them. Listen. He is calling you by name. Listen and then go find Him. He *promises* to be found! Hide and seek with Jesus is awesome!

As ministry leaders we lead by example. There is no other way to lead. *I believe that at least some of our week needs to be in selfless service to others who can do nothing for us or the ministries we serve.* We must walk the talk. Christian leaders follow Christ to hurting people, and as we do, our hearts will continually be renewed and other leaders in the ministry will close in around the Shepherd, listening and following Him. We will encourage each other. The least will be loved, our Father will be glorified, the ministry will be transformed, and we will burn with pure, Holy Spirit power. Praise be to God for this abundant life!

And, once we begin entering into the incredible adventure the Lord has for *us*, it changes how we encourage others within the church to discover and follow what God has for *them*.

Chapter 6

But, as it is written, "What no eye has seen, nor ear heard,
nor the heart of man imagined, what God has prepared for
those who love him"—these things God has revealed to us
through the Spirit. For the Spirit searches everything,
even the depths of God.

1 CORINTHIANS 2:9-10

At one point, Light of Christ needed a new coordinator for our youth ministry, so instead of looking outside our church walls for a person, we placed an announcement in our church bulletin. This was in response to a radical principle I learned from Pastor Barnett about how Phoenix First Assembly only chose people from within their own church for ministry leadership positions in the church. Just like the Lord answered the widow's need through something already in her house, all we need as pastors is already in our house.

This is the central principle: for every Spirit-led ministry, the leader is already present. In congregations, the pastor is the *only* exception to this principle, as he will probably come from outside the ministry. However, as ministry leaders, we need to pray without ceasing, seeking the Spirit's discernment on God's choices for leadership. We need to be disciples of Jesus first, encourage others in their discipleship second, and then prayerfully and patiently wait for the Spirit to bring the next ministry leader forward. The ministry waits for the leader. The worst thing we can do is force someone into a ministry that is not God's will because of impatience to fill a slot. It takes patience and prayer. Then more patience and more prayer. When the Lord brings the called person forward and he or she begins to serve, I promise that you will praise Him for teaching you to be patient.

As we were patiently praying for our youth ministry, I received a call from Paula Cunkelman. She and her husband Wade, a couple in their fifties, had been at Light of Christ since its very first service. She had previously worked with my wife Linda with the youth, and with Dave as a Sunday school teacher. I knew Paula had a heart for youth, stemming from many years back when a youth pastor was instrumental in helping her kids, then adolescents, deal with her divorce from their father.

"I think God wants me to do this," she said, "and I have no idea why. I just hear the Lord keep telling me, 'You love the youth. You've been through a lot; your kids have been through a lot. You should do it!'"

"Paula, you would be great!" I said.

Her candidacy was made known to the board. We prayed about it, discussed it, and approved her for the position. I directed her to get all of the parents and kids together for a meal and meeting after church and see what God wanted to do. I then added, "Now, I'm not going to be there. You don't need me. If I'm there, people are going to look to me for direction. But I don't know what God has for this ministry. You'll work that out together with them, and the Holy Spirit will be there to direct you. You simply coordinate getting everyone together for prayer and discussion. God will do the rest."

"It was the greatest meeting I've ever been in,"
she said, unable to hide her joyful surprise.

As the meeting got ready to begin, I was in my office when Paula peeked around the door.

"Okay, pastor, we're about to start," she said. "I was wondering if you could come in and say the opening prayer, and maybe answer any questions from anyone."

I looked up at her from my desk chair. "Nope. Can't do it, Paula."

She looked around, clearly noting that I didn't seem to have anything to do and was in no hurry. "Why? Do you have something else planned?"

"No. Not a thing in the world." She smiled. "Paula, you'll be *fine*. Jesus is with you. Pray for the Spirit's guidance, and see what He does. Don't worry." I stood, walked over to her, and took her hands in mine and prayed for her. She then walked away toward the meeting—and I left out the back door to go home.

Four hours later, I gave her a call. "What was it like?" I asked.

"It was the greatest meeting I've ever been in," she said, unable to hide her joyful surprise. "Everyone was so enthusiastic. We have the whole year planned out. Parents are volunteering and the kids are excited about ministry."

Paula later said, "Organization is my thing, but being in charge of the spiritual side of it, leading and preparing the studies—I was going to be on my own." But she said my reminder that the Holy Spirit was going to lead her made all of the difference at the meeting. "I talked about how it was important for them as parents to be involved in the work for their youth and to volunteer. I talked about what I saw the youth becoming—and they were ready to be a part of it. Everything flowed so easily. I thought, 'Yeah, I just need to get out of God's way.'"

Paula went on to serve as youth coordinator for the next five years. She now oversees hospitality and works in the children's ministry. Of that time with the youth, Paula said God showed her that "no matter what generation you are, there's always a common bond, and that as long as you allow God to be in control, you can always have guidance for the youth and learn from the youth. Their struggles were real, but their hearts were so open to learn from the Lord."

In regards to service-oriented activities, the youth participated in such ministries as the Mexico mission trips and initiatives to help Feed My Starving Children. Paula said she and her husband Wade tried to get the young people "outside of themselves and to realize that as blessed as they are, they have so much to give, and that they need to give out of the blessings they have received." Wade added that in youth ministry and any other service to Christ that "it's always important to keep the channels open between you and God in prayer, accepting His way instead of trying to force your way on things." I couldn't have said it better myself.

Along with the board's directive and its amazing impact on me and on the church, that eight month period brought one more blessing that couldn't have been more personal or surprising. Just after that pivotal board meeting in April, my wife and I left the United States and went to St. Petersburg, Russia—to adopt our oldest son. It all started nine months earlier when a group of twenty-nine children from orphanages in Russia were brought to Arizona for a five-week American experience. During this time, host families housed the children, and four families from Light of Christ, including mine, participated. The program's goal was not explicitly adoption; the orphans benefitted greatly from the opportunity to come to the United States and have contact with the people and the culture here. Adoption, however, was an option for any family and child who agreed to it.

There was one boy named Ilya Fedorovich who immediately caught Linda's eye. In English, his name translates Elijah Theodore. Theodore is also the name of my father and brother. Quite the coincidence!

"You better keep me away from that one," she warned. "There's something about him."

I saw it, too, and though it had been three years since we had our last child, neither one of us were considering adoption. After all, we had three children already with differing origins. The first two, our twin boys, were birthed by Linda after a frozen embryo transfer procedure; our third, a daughter, was conceived and birthed naturally after the doctors had said it wasn't possible. Yet God's plans are not ours, are they? We continued to be drawn to Elijah, but each time we asked for the opportunity to have him live in our home for a few days, another host family already had him. We patiently waited for the Lord's will to be done.

Finally, just four days before all of the orphans were scheduled to be flown back to Russia, we couldn't take it any longer. We *had* to know if Elijah was our son! By then, he was staying with one of the Russian staff, so we asked again if he could stay with us. The staff person was hesitant. Elijah did not want to stay with anymore families. He had already been in three homes, and all three families had decided they were not interested in adopting him. He was understandably done with the whole process and just wanted to return to Russia. Hearing the urgency in my voice, though, the person relented and convinced Elijah to come stay with us. It was Wednesday when we were able to pick him up and bring him home. All the way there and all the way back home, Linda and I prayed, "Lord, you already know what you want. Just make it clear to us."

Upon arrival at our home, Elijah started playing with our children right away. Elijah was eight, the twins were five, and our daughter was two—but the age and culture differences seemed non-existent. They got along so well, so naturally. It was a fun, delightful day, and Elijah seemed to love it even though the kids did not know a word of each other's languages. Linda and I were beginning to get cold chills: "Is this really happening? Lord, are you serious!" After a lot of prayer on Wednesday evening, Linda and I gathered our children together on Thursday afternoon while Elijah was away for an activity with the other children from Russia. We knew we'd be picking him up again before dinner, and then he'd be with us the remainder of the time before he was due to return to St. Petersburg.

I looked at Linda expectantly and then spoke. "We want to run something by you. We're wondering if God might want Elijah to be a part of our family. What do you think? Is he supposed to be your brother?"

All three of our kids started jumping—literally—for joy! "Woo-hoo!" "Absolutely!" "That will be awesome!" "Another brother!"

With the wishes of our children clear, now all we had to do was make sure Elijah wanted to be part of our family. We were unable to get in touch with a translator to ask Elijah if he wanted to be our son. We actually had to wait three more days, until Sunday morning at a nearby church parking lot where all of the children were being dropped off for their return trip to Russia, before a translator was available. We were on pins and needles wondering how Elijah was going to respond. To make matters more nerve wracking, the translator was late! I had to leave to get ready for our church's worship services at a school twenty minutes away, so I wasn't there when Linda, the translator, and Elijah finally met.

Linda said the three of them stepped away from the larger group, and her words were translated to Elijah: "Ilya, we have talked about this as a family, and we have prayed about it, and we would love it if you would come and be part of our family here in America."

This precious boy looked from the translator to Linda and said one word.

The translator interpreted. "Forever?"

Linda began to cry, nodded her head, and replied, "Yes. *Forever.*"

Elijah smiled, nodded, gave her a hug, and ran off to be with his friends from the orphanage.

At the school, I was up front on the platform leading the service, but my mind was elsewhere. *Did Elijah say "yes?"* Moments later, I saw Linda come in the back doors. She simply gave me a "thumbs up" gesture—and my heart and spirit rejoiced. I made no announcement to the congregation; I felt it was premature to say anything knowing that the adoption process was still ahead of us. But I wanted to scream it from the rooftops! I don't remember anything about the worship service that day except a blur of utter joy.

Matter of fact, if I am actually listening to and following Jesus, the first ones to receive the Holy Spirit blessings pouring out of me will be my family.

In the end, the three other Light of Christ families who took in an orphan ended up adopting as well. And, thanks to the board's mandate, upon our return from Russia with our new son, I had precious, irreplaceable time to spend getting to know Elijah. By the time our first Christmas with him arrived, he was fully immersed in American culture. My parents were over on Christmas Eve when my dad decided to log onto the

Internet site that was tracking Santa's travels around the globe. He called Elijah over to him. "Look!" he said, pointing to the screen. "Santa Claus is over Russia!" Elijah just stared at the monitor in bewilderment. His expression communicated a great deal of confusion. He simply asked, "Why?" We later learned that Santa had never visited Elijah when he was in Russia, so he simply wondered what had changed!

I'm not sure how I forgot this, but our Father cares about *everything* in my life, including my home life. How can I possibly convince myself I am following Jesus while ignoring my family? How is it that I could micromanage everyone in ministry, be stunningly impatient with my family, spend countless hours at work, try to control almost every facet of the ministry as though it were mine to control, be on the verge of complete burnout, and do it all in the name of Jesus? What is wrong with this picture and how is it *possible* that I didn't see it?

Matter of fact, if I am actually listening to and following Jesus, the first ones to receive the Holy Spirit blessings pouring out of me will be my family.

Follow Jesus, dear brothers and sisters in Christ. Listen to Him. He knows what you need to hear. Walk with Him. He never ran anywhere. Give your burdens to Him. He alone can carry them. Give Him back His church. He never signed it over to you. Let Him love you to life. He is the only One who can. It is enough. Oh, how he will use your witness! He will bless us all through you. Your ministry, your family and your life will never be the same.

Joy and peace was our portion as the new year dawned, and I was enthusiastically ready to continue to, as Dave had said, "go and find out" what it meant to live as the spiritual leader of the church and move forward in my personal journey of discipleship with the Lord. Good thing, too, because it was about to take a turn into an area of ministry that was completely unexpected and life-transforming—and was going to deliver another blow to my ego, knocking me completely off my high horse. All from the humble witness of a beautiful man.

✢

It's funny. Even in the midst of incredible blessing and times of reinforced humility in our relationship with Jesus, we can still be way too big for our britches.

Such was the case for me as I started the next year still enjoying the freedom of the board's mandate. I was driving one afternoon just praying in my car and listening for the Lord's voice when I found myself near the Archstone Care Center on Pecos Road in Chandler. I periodically visited with the father of one of our church's families who resided there, but on this day I was being told by the Spirit of God to stop there and go inside. The problem was I didn't know why God wanted me to do it.

I got out of the car and went inside the main lobby. It was as inviting as a hotel, with soft lighting and plush furniture arranged neatly in a large common area flanked on one side by the receptionist's desk. I walked over to the woman behind the counter.

"Hi there! I'm Pastor Moe from a church in the neighborhood. I'm not sure, but I think I'm supposed to do something here."

Not exactly an insightful greeting, and not even spoken in the form of a question. But she knew how to best reply. "Well, let me call our activities director. Please wait right here."

I selected a spot on one of the comfy couches and was met moments later by Archstone's activities director. She looked like she was pretty busy. I repeated my well-worded message, and she froze. Her eyes became wide as saucers. "Oh my goodness!" she exclaimed. "Do you have some time to come to my office to sit and talk?"

"Absolutely," I responded. *I have nowhere else to go, anyway. I've got all the time in the world.*

Once in her office, the director told me about a gentleman named Floyd who for years had been providing a worship service for the residents at Archstone every Thursday morning at ten o'clock, but now had to step down to move back to Minnesota. He was leaving after the next service. "We need someone to take over," she said. "The service means so much to our residents." She leaned closer. "I have already contacted thirty churches in this area. All of them said they can't help us."

My inner voice chimed in, *Well, that's because they're not as holy as I am.* Thank the Lord that thing wasn't audible! Later He chastised me: "Holy? Yeah, it could be that, *Skippy*—or it might be that I had this ministry set aside just for you."

"I guess that's what I am supposed to do," I told her confidently. "I'm free on Thursday mornings and will be glad to lead the service for you." Thrilled, she gave me Floyd's phone number and I contacted him later that afternoon from my office. We coordinated to be back at Archstone two days later on Thursday so he could pass the proverbial baton to me. I also found out that Floyd was ninety-one years old and actually not a pastor at all, but simply called himself "a servant of Jesus."

That's awesome! my inner voice said. *With me there, now they're going to get a polished presentation, a professional service. They are in for such a treat!* As I was thinking about all that I was going to do for the good people of Archstone, one of our longtime members, Ruby Rivinius, came up to my open office door.

"Pastor, do you have a few minutes?"

"Yeah, Ruby," I said. "What have you got?"

She said, "I don't even want to be here."

I almost laughed but restrained myself. She seemed serious. "What?"

"I just feel like God wants me to talk to you," she continued, "but I didn't want to come, because you always ask the same thing."

"What is that?"

"You always say, 'How's your walk with our Heavenly Father? Because if that's strong, everything else is going to be okay,' and I didn't want to hear it."

I leaned back in my chair. "Well, guess what? I'm not going to say that to you today."

"Really?" she quizzed.

"No, because I already know why you're here."

"You do?" Ruby's eyebrows arched upward.

"Yep. You're supposed to come help me with a weekly worship service at a nursing home starting this Thursday."

She stood still and stared straight in front of her. After a long silence, she said, "Well, I do love old people!"

So that's how it came to be that Ruby and I headed over to Archstone on Thursday morning to meet up with Floyd and provide the pastor's touch needed to take the service to the next level. I had on my suit and tie, Ruby was in her Sunday best, and we even had one page bulletins so the residents could follow along with the service. We arrived about a half-hour early, and as the people started filtering in I said hello, shook hands, and gave each person a bulletin. About a quarter 'til ten, Floyd still hadn't arrived. Then it hit ten 'til. Five 'til. The service was about to start. I looked at Ruby and whispered, "Where *is* this guy?"

What do you expect? the inner voice said. *He's not a professional.*

At precisely 10:03 a.m., in walked Floyd—an absolute angel of God! The residents, all slouched and sad in their wheelchairs, perked up, sat about four inches higher than they had been, and their eyes started to dance as smiles curled across their faces. Floyd went to each person, hugging necks and kissing cheeks. He knew each one by name.

And I just started to cry as the Lord's loving conviction washed over me. *Oh, Heavenly Father,* I prayed. *Please forgive me for my ridiculous arrogance. If you can just keep things here at this level, and allow me to be part of it, that will be beautiful.*

People talk about "leaving a legacy."
Is *everything* in this life about me,
even when I am no longer here?

Pride is the chief obstacle to what the Holy Spirit wants to accomplish in us and through us. The Holy Spirit wants to take control of our lives and help us to learn obedience, all the while giving *all* glory, honor, and praise to God. Yet pride screams, "No!" to all of this. If you admit in your heart right now that you struggle with pride, thank you for being honest. I struggle with that plank of pride and self-righteousness growing out of my eye every single day. The temptation is to become greater while speaking less and less about Jesus; leading instead of following; speaking without listening first. It was my greatest struggle in writing this book. The issue was this: is it possible to write a book that gives God all of the glory? I don't know the answer to that question—but I hope so.

The biblical references to the evils of pride are far too many to list. Here is a sampling from the book of Proverbs: "When pride comes, then comes disgrace, but with the humble is wisdom." (Proverbs 11:2); "Pride goes before destruction, and a haughty spirit before a fall." (Proverbs16: 18); "One's pride will bring him low, but he who is lowly in spirit will obtain honor." (Proverbs 29: 23) What was Jesus trying to break through with His numerous confrontations with the Pharisees and Sadducees if not their pride?

Scripture tells us there are two areas about which we are allowed to boast: 1) "Let the one who boasts, boast in the Lord." (2 Corinthians 10: 17); 2) "If I must boast, I will boast of the things that show my weakness." (2 Corinthians 11: 30) I can do nothing without Him. He can do 99.999999 percent of what He planned without me. I am nothing. He is everything. And yet the great and glorious news is He still *chose* me—sinful, broken, selfish, seemingly insignificant little old me. He has chosen me to be a very small part of what He is doing, and He chose you, too! Praise be to God! Boast about Him and the things that show your weakness, and rest in the loving, joyful freedom that you are chosen.

It kind of cracks me up how focusing on self in this worldly culture is encouraged even after we are gone. People talk about "leaving a legacy." Is *everything* in this life about me, even when I am no longer here? Truth be told, my legacy is to be forgotten. This may be hard to digest in a narcissistic culture where people actually post pictures of what they had for breakfast (*really?*), but at least for me, my legacy is to be forgotten. My family will remember me for a couple generations, but that's about it. And you know what? That's okay. I owe Jesus everything. My life is no longer about me. Jesus sets me *free* from me. My life is about Him. He died so I might live. I don't know about you, but I want to live! I want to live for Him. I want to shine my light so our Father will be glorified! I want people to know the name of Jesus. Who cares if they know our names? Jesus knows our names. He calls us by name to follow Him. That is more than enough. We have a place in His plan. Thank you, Lord!

We are not alone in this ongoing, daily struggle with pride. It is universal.

"Leaders who fail to prune their pride will meet demise," leadership expert John C. Maxwell said. "That's not a guess, it's a guarantee. With pride, it's not a matter of 'if' we will fall, but 'when.' There are no exceptions." Great preacher Charles Spurgeon added: "Revenge, lust, ambition, pride, and self-will are too often exalted as the gods of man's idolatry; while holiness, peace, contentment, and humility are viewed as unworthy of a serious thought."

Author and Christian apologist C.S. Lewis said, "Pride gets no pleasure out of having something, only out of having more of it than the next man ... It is the comparison that makes you proud: the pleasure of being above the rest. Once the element of competition is gone, pride is gone." He also said, "Through pride the devil became the devil. Pride leads to every vice; it's the complete anti-God state of mind."

Pride brings out the absolute worst in us. Pride produces arrogance and envy. Pride has an excuse for every sin. Pride will never apologize. Pride refuses to listen. Pride makes everything a competition. Pride must win and leaves a wake of brokenness and bitterness. And humility? When our Heavenly Father humbles us and then teaches us how to walk in Holy Spirit humility, He brings out that which is unique, beautiful, gracious, and even funny in us. It is amazing how playful humor flows when we are at peace with our Lord, ourselves, and each other.

John Bunyan was a seventeenth century English writer and Baptist preacher best remembered as the author of *The Pilgrim's Progress*. After the restoration of the monarch, when the freedom to preach was curtailed, Bunyan was arrested and spent the next twelve years in jail as he refused to give up preaching. During this time he wrote a spiritual autobiography, *Grace Abounding to the Chief of Sinners*. He was a power-ful preacher, but remained a very humble man. One of my favorite stories of Bunyan was when, after hearing his message, an admirer approached him and exclaimed, "It was such a sweet sermon." To which Bunyan replied, "You need not remind me of that; for the devil told me of it before I was out of the pulpit."

American Catholic writer Thomas Merton said, "Pride makes us arti-ficial and humility makes us real." Pastor Francis Chan pointed out that "a person who is obsessed with Jesus knows that the sin of pride is always a battle. Obsessed people know that you can never be 'humble enough,' and so they seek to make themselves less known and Christ more known." Perhaps songwriter and musician Mac Davis was attempting to express the same thought, if in a roundabout way, when he coined, "Oh Lord, it's hard to be humble / when you're perfect in every way / I can't wait to look in the mirror / Cause I get better looking each day / Oh Lord, it's hard to be humble / but I'm doing the best that I can."

Besides, it is so much easier to walk in humility, avoid the limelight, and give God all of the glory! Pastor Brian Steele, director of the Phoenix Dream Center, once offered to ask a television crew he knew well to do a story on our congregation at Light of Christ to be broadcast over the entire Valley of the Sun and a potential audience of three million people! My mind immediately began whirring with the immense possibilities. *Here is my chance! The beginning of my television ministry. Watch out, world, here I come! Of course, I will need to get hair plugs, spend some time in the tanning booth, get my teeth capped, and drop at least twenty pounds. Wait! That's a lot of work.* These thoughts actually ran through my mind! I laughed and the Lord gave me peace with my answer. "I really appre-ciate that, Brian. I really do. But our place is simply in the background supporting all of you. It is our joy." Pastor Brian wanted to thank us for our partnership. Praise God! His offer was thanks enough.

Honestly, I had been chasing personal recognition from others my whole life. The Spirit gave me wisdom about myself. He gave me the grace to give up the chase. *Please understand* that I am not telling you what to do; only what I sensed the Lord wanted me to do. It may be that you are humble enough to have a worldwide ministry and give God all of the glory. I don't believe I am there yet. There is incredible freedom in staying in the background!

The Lord gently removed that plank of pride and judgment from my eye by the witness and love of His humble servant, Floyd. He indeed passed the baton to my hands that were now properly trembling with holy reverence and respect for this mighty man of God who obviously meant so much to this community of people.

I had to know more about this brother in Christ. In *genuine* humility, I talked to him later and learned a bit of his story. He had started the ministry at Archstone twenty-five years earlier when his wife was a resident there and he led a Bible study for her and two other ladies. He was a spry sixty-six year old then and, as he put it, "They all died but I kept coming." He started going room to room praying with folks and inviting them to attend. When he was seventy-three, Floyd said he felt led by the Spirit that the group needed to start singing songs—so he taught himself how to play the piano! I witnessed at the service we shared that he could really jam those old songs. He didn't need any sheet music. He had the songs memorized. And I thought I would improve the service?

Thank you, Lord Jesus, for your grace, patience, and gentle correction! Thank you for your beautiful servant, Floyd.

Chapter 7

Do not neglect to show hospitality to strangers,
for thereby some have entertained angels unawares.
HEBREWS 13:2

M eeting Floyd was just the beginning. We were completely unaware of the miraculous people of faith who resided in the care facilities. The Lord brought us to them—or perhaps He brought them to us.

With the powerful precedent of a Holy Spirit-filled worship service in full gear thanks to Floyd listening to Jesus and following Him, Ruby and I returned to Archstone every Thursday. Over time we were joined by other volunteers from Light of Christ. We discovered that the residents especially missed the music Floyd had provided for so long, so I put the piano lessons my parents had lovingly forced upon me as a child to good use. I worked on the old songs, practicing for hours to hone skills I hadn't exercised since I was a boy. It wasn't easy, but I was able to do passable renditions of sacred hymns such as "How Great Thou Art," "What a Friend We Have in Jesus," and "Amazing Grace."

I say "passable" because on the days my mother, who accompanied Sunday morning worship for over forty years, joined us for the service and played the piano, it was clear she was the crowd favorite at tickling the ivories. "Can you have her come every week?" was a question I fielded from more than one resident. *Humility everywhere!* Regardless, the Lord used the music in powerful ways. In one service, one of the residents who we hadn't seen move in her chair for months suddenly stood up and started clapping when we played and sang "Jesus Loves Me." It's those wonderful traditional songs that most touched the hearts of those precious Archstone residents, and they in return certainly plucked at our heartstrings.

I believe the Lord had been preparing me for this ministry, not just because of my music background, but because one of the people I admire the most lived the last eight years of her life in a nursing home. My dear grandmother Benna was a light to me! At her funeral, the preacher said, "What do you do when you can't do anything? You can pray like Benna." And pray she did! This mighty woman of God had a prayer list of well over one hundred people. Every day she carried all of us by name to the throne of our Heavenly Father. She prayed for the Spirit to guide and direct us. She prayed for the love of the Lord to fill us. She prayed for our Heavenly Father to protect us and use us to care for others. She was a prayer warrior throughout all of her years in the care facility.

Yet the one thing she was unable to do was make it to church on Sunday mornings. She could watch various worship services on television, and her pastor visited her when he could, but she was never again able to enter our Father's house and celebrate with her church family. It broke my heart. But here's the thing: "And we know that for those who love God all things work together for good, for those who are called according to his purpose." (Romans 8:28) The Lord takes our broken hearts from yesterday and heals and blesses them for ministry today and tomorrow. Do you have a broken heart from your past? It may give you direction on where Jesus will lead you to serve today and into the future.

Joan, you are such a blessing to us all.
I'll see you on the other side.

The Lord has given me a strong conviction that if these beautiful people cannot come to church, then the church must come to them. Thank you, Lord—and thank you, Grandma Benna, for your heart of prayer! What is the result today? We have the honor of bringing a worship service to three different care facilities every week. We can never thank God enough for the hundreds of precious brothers and sisters we have had the privilege of knowing and loving through the nursing home ministry. I used to visit four shut-ins a month. Now I have the *joy* of worshipping with over seventy incredible, shut-in children of God every week.

I particularly remember Joan. Joan had such a heart of love for God and people. She knew all the other residents at Archstone. She knew who was sick, who needed special prayers, who was in the hospital, and who had been released to their earthly or their heavenly home. She was a light shining in the darkness.

One Thanksgiving Day she told me that it was her sixty-eighth anniversary.

"Sixty-eighth anniversary? Of what?" I asked.

"Of the last time I walked," she responded. "It was Thanksgiving and I was twenty-one years old when, while I was helping my sister do the dishes, I felt an intense pain down my right side. We went to the hospital the next day, and I was diagnosed with polio." I gasped, but she smiled. "But you know what? Since that day, Jesus has been so beautiful to me. He's given me a faithful family and He's always provided for me."

Several months after that conversation, I arrived fifteen minutes early for the worship service at Archstone. Our volunteers always arrived early, but not me. For some reason I did that day. I quickly discovered why. One of our volunteers informed me that Joan was close to death. "Can you go in before worship and see her?"

I did, of course, and found her daughter and son-in-law at her bedside. Joan was unconscious. I sat and visited with her family about what a blessing Joan had been to all of us. I then prayed for them and for her. Before leaving, I said, "Joan, you are such a blessing to us all. I'll see you on the other side. You have done such a beautiful work here. Well done! God bless you, sister. I love you. We all love you." Only ten minutes into the service, we were informed that Joan had crossed over and was in Heaven. It immediately occurred to me that if I had not arrived early, I would not have had that precious time with Joan and her family. God is good.

As you'd imagine, the residents there are used to death. It is a constant companion. There was sadness but also great joy. Joan's suffering was now over! No more medications, no more wheelchairs. I believe she is dancing in heaven right now, and cheering us on! We praised and thanked Jesus for Joan, and then continued on with the service.

Along with the somber occasions came moments of delightful levity. While taking prayer requests one day, James lifted his hand. I thought I knew what was coming. James always asked for the same things: healing for his conditions caused by stroke, and for better dreams. That's understandable for a man in his mid-eighties. This time, though, he had a different need piercing his heart.

"Pastor Moe," he said nice and loud. "I feel lonely and I want a wife. I want you to pray for God to bring me a wife!"

It took me a second to get my bearings. "Excuse me, James?" I said.

He repeated his request, smiling from ear to ear, "I said I want you to pray for the Heavenly Father to bring me a wife! I want a wife!"

I wasn't exactly sure how to respond, but I didn't have to. Up front, Lucille raised her hand and her voice, "Well, I'm available. But I'm not getting married without a ring!"

And then everything broke loose! We laughed so hard we were crying. Well, probably half of us were laughing. The other half can hardly hear, so they were asking each other, "What did he say?"

Another day I preached about how easily I get off track from following the Lord. I asked the rhetorical question, "What is wrong with me?" Before I could continue, a playful brother in Christ named Brad smiled and asked, "Do you want a list?" I told him he was on my list now!

The joy of the Lord is everywhere at these services with these precious people. They are genuine with the same heartaches and humor as anyone else. They are also people of sweet, childlike faith. All they want is Jesus. They help us know Him better, too. Some of them know Jesus very well. With others, we have the joy of introducing them to Him. These beautiful children of God also desire a family of faith around them. Brothers and sisters who love them and they get to love in return!

I'll never forget a dear sister in Christ who began attending worship at Light of Christ. She succinctly told me one day, "No one needs a church, but everyone needs a church family." Yes! In family we not only receive love..We also pour out love to others. And the more we pour out, the more our Father pours in.

Just ask Ruby. For years, she had struggled with depression. She'd been to doctors and therapists and none seemed to have the solution for her despondency. About eight weeks after we'd started the weekly ministry at Archstone, the board approved the purchase of large print Bibles that Ruby helped give out as a gift to the folks at the nursing home. They were so appreciative and had already grown to love Ruby's presence at the services. One Sunday morning at Light of Christ Church, we showed a PowerPoint presentation of the Bibles being handed out to the residents. Ruby got up on the platform and took the congregation through the presentation and spoke of the remarkable people at Archstone. It was apparent to all how much love and joy Ruby had caring for these precious people. When Ruby was finished she stepped down to take her seat in the congregation. Moments later, with my sermon well underway, Ruby started waving at me.

"I'm sorry, Ruby," I said. "Did you have something to add?"

She stood and proclaimed, loudly and joyfully, "I used to suffer with depression before going to Archstone. I haven't had a single day of depression since!"

I finished my sermon, but I really didn't have to. Jesus had already been mightily glorified through her brief but potent testimony of God's miraculous power.

All I can tell you is this: if you want to see miracles—starting with the Lord filling your heart with so much love you feel you will burst—may I recommend the nursing homes in your community? It will keep you grounded with Jesus as He shines His light through you. Use your gifts to love those precious children of God. What you pour out, the Holy Spirit will multiply and pour back into you. Try to outpour the Holy Spirit. I triple dog dare you! God gets the glory, hurting people are loved and encouraged, and we are renewed as our Father rewards us with joy!

✧

I heard a sermon thirty years ago with an image that has never left my mind. The preacher reached as high as he could and then pointing down while lowering his hand, he said, "Impression without expression (hands moving out to the side) leads to depression." When we are impressed with the power, love, peace, and joy of the Holy Spirit coming into us, we must pour that out to others! The Holy Spirit pours power and love to me to go *through* me. It was never meant to simply fill me up, or for me to hoard all to myself. We are created to serve! This is intricately connected with what we proclaim from the pulpit.

I believe that Holy Spirit filled preaching, as blessed and beautiful as that is, is only the beginning. Our preaching may be quite powerful and the Spirit may be motivating people to pour into others like never before—but it is then essential that we offer people as many *opportunities* to pour into others as possible. Are we giving people numerous ways to get involved, or challenging them to pray about starting something new, that will truly make a difference in people's lives? If not, and if the highlight of their week is the Sunday morning experience, the rest of their week will be depressed by comparison. That's tragic, because there are already too many broken, hurting, lonely, and depressed people in this world.

Spirit-filled preaching is to challenge people to allow the Spirit full control of their lives, which leads to loving, self-sacrificing *action*. This is why the Lord didn't take us to Heaven immediately upon our acceptance of His salvation: there is work to do! Getting us out of our own way so our Father can use us for His purposes is the whole point of sanctification. Spirit-filled preaching should ignite that childlike, adventurous faith the Lord has placed within us. Spirit-filled preaching, if it gets people out of the boat to follow Jesus, challenges them to believe in the miraculous life they have always desired. Spirit-filled preaching gets the *preacher* out of the way so our Father can speak directly to His children with words that encourage, love, challenge, comfort, and empower us all. Spirit-filled preaching faces fear with Holy Spirit power—and blows right through it!

Far from producing depressed people, the Lord will *bring us to depressed and hurting* people to love them the way He loves them. Once again, we must walk this talk. Without the walk, the words don't get very far.

Ideally, Spirit-filled preaching produces Spirit-filled listeners. The highlight of the week will not be the Sunday morning worship service. It will be the countless acts of love the Holy Spirit pours through us over the rest of the week as God's ambassadors in His world. Sunday morning then becomes a time to praise God for choosing us to be a very small part of His ongoing rescue mission, as we praise Him for what He has done, is doing, and will do through our lives. To God be all the glory, now and forever!

> Am listening to Jesus, following
> Jesus, and living for Jesus? Am I truly
> saved for all eternity as well as saved
> from a selfish, small life *today*?

As we leave the worship filled with the Spirit, we follow Jesus into a hurting, helpless, hopeless world to live the adventure we were created to live—and what an adventure it is! When we dive in and love Jesus by serving others, there is also no better way to spend our time or our treasure. If we are blessed with financial means, praise God! It is a gift from God. Does anyone give gifts so the other person feels guilty? Perhaps, but certainly not our Heavenly Father. He gave us our financial blessings. But remember, "From everyone who has been given much, much will be demanded; and from the one who has been entrusted with much, much more will be asked." (Luke 12: 48 NIV) We praise Him both for the financial provision *and* the responsibility that comes with it. They are *both* blessings!

Thank you, dear Father, that you have so financially blessed us that we can generously, joyfully give back to you and your work in the world. We owe you everything. We will be like the Macedonian church that *begged* to be allowed to contribute and help others, although they (unlike us) were very poor (2 Corinthians 8).

Caring for the helpless, hopeless, lonely, and lost happens *automatically* when we become Spirit-fed and Spirit-led, just like our Lord's parable of the sheep and goats in Matthew 25:31-46. Neither the sheep nor the goats knew that anything remarkable had happened. Both called Jesus "Lord," but one group automatically cared for the least. The other automatically did not. Considering one group was saved and the other lost for eternity, this parable should get our full attention. Am I listening to Jesus, following Jesus, and living for Jesus? Am I truly saved for all eternity as well as saved from a selfish, small life *today*? Is the Holy Spirit leading and empowering me? Is the Lord living in my heart? If so, I will follow Jesus and automatically serve others. He will use my example to lead others.

I remember that we were driving one night on a family vacation, and Linda was seated between Elijah and Micah in the back seat. Elijah had been with us less than a year, but he was already fluent in English. The three of them were looking at the stars and discussing how awesome God is. Then Elijah asked, "How do we *know* God exists?" Linda was about to answer when Micah said, "Of course, God exists. I mean, we all have hearts. That proves that God exists, because the only reason we have a heart is for God to live in it." Yes, Lord! And when He takes up residency, our hearts change.

James 1:27 declares, "Religion that is pure and undefiled before God, the Father, is this: to visit orphans and widows in their affliction, and to keep oneself unstained from the world." Nursing home outreaches such as the ones we have at Archstone, Desert Cove and Chandler HealthCare are just a few of many ways God desires us as His church to engage in servant ministry. The people who join Light of Christ will generally say it is for one of a few reasons: the incredible love and peace they experience, our relentless focus upon God's Word and listening to Jesus, or the servant ministries. We always challenge them to allow the Spirit to create in them a new heart as well: the heart of Jesus.

In Christian ministry, it's a constant temptation for us to take on worldly means to achieve greater numbers, but those means will only have worldly ends, and I believe the Lord will not bless it. Some may say, "But look at how many people are going to that church! Perhaps raffling off a car is the way to go." I truly believe attendance numbers mean nothing. Faithfulness (doing what God wants the way He wants it done) is everything. There are great servant ministries that are obedient, have thousands of people in attendance (like Phoenix First Assembly), and are blessed by God with joy. There are also great servant ministries that are obedient, have two dozen or so people in attendance (like Floyd leading worship for decades at Archstone), and are blessed by God with joy. What our Father is looking for is obedience, and His reward is joy. Pastor Wurmbrand wrote that often he was overwhelmed with the joy of the Lord while he was in solitary confinement in a communist prison. The Lord rewarded his obedience with joy. *Nothing* can compare with the joy of the Lord. We know when we have it, and we know when we don't.

Besides, the subject matter is so important (Jesus and eternal life) that entertaining people is an insult! When was the last time you went to your doctor and he or she said, "Before I get to the results of your tests, I would like to have my assistant show you a card trick." I always tell people that if they want to be entertained, there's a movie theater right down the street. Hollywood studios are paying billions of dollars to entertain us. Professional athletes are getting tens of millions of dollars a year to entertain us. Don't get me started on the video game industry. People are inundated with entertainment everywhere they turn. All they *need* is Jesus. Are we giving them the only One they need, the Lover of their soul? Heaven help us if Christian ministries *fail* to give them Jesus! Christian ministry should be the one place on Earth where focusing on Jesus is guaranteed. Christ said, "And I, when I am lifted up from the earth, will draw all people to myself." (John 12:32) This is our Lord's promise. Christ dying for us draws us to Him. Lift Him up. Point everyone to Him. His love, sacrifice, patience, forgiveness, and gentleness will draw *everyone* to Himself through the power of the Holy Spirit.

Pastor Barnett said of church attendance, "Whatever brings them there will keep them there." That means if you're relying on entertainment to get people to your church, you better keep entertaining them. I don't know about you, but I didn't go into the entertainment business. Imagine the difference when it's nothing but our Father's love, Christ crucified, that we lift up! Imagine if it is the prayers of the faithful for the Lord to send us broken, hurting people that "brings them there." Church is a place to come to pray, praise, learn, experience healing, receive salvation and hope, care for each other, and then follow Jesus back out into the world to serve. It is our Father's house—and it is meant to be set apart from worldliness.

Consider how furious our Lord was to witness what happened in the temple courts in Jerusalem. When it was almost time for the Jewish Passover, He went to the temple and "found those who were selling oxen and sheep and pigeons, and the money-changers sitting there. And making a whip of cords, he drove them all out of the temple, with the sheep and oxen. And he poured out the coins of the money-changers and overturned their tables. And he told those who sold the pigeons, 'Take these things away; do not make my Father's house a house of trade!' His disciples remembered that it was written, 'Zeal for your house will consume me.'" (John 2:14b-17)

I believe we get an insight into a person's soul when we realize what really sets them off. According to the Bible, *nothing* infuriated Jesus more than people turning His Father's house into something it was never meant to be. He made a whip, for crying out loud! We must all resist the temptation to make our ministries worldly, no matter how others try and justify it. The house of God is a sacred, holy place where souls are saved, the broken are healed, the lonely find family, and God gets all the glory. It is a sanctuary from the world. It is where Jesus *alone* is lifted up and the Spirit brings God's children home. Would Jesus need to make a whip and chase me out of our Father's house at Light of Christ, at least until the Spirit got me back on track?

This is another of the unexpected blessings with nursing home ministries: God continually transforms our minds. (Romans 12:1-2) The ministry is so simple and so very clear. All these precious people need is

Jesus and His love. We are not there to fix them or their problems. Nor are we there to entertain them. We are simply there to allow the love of Jesus to flow through us to them. Guess what? The Lord has shown us this is precisely what Sunday morning worship should be as well! The truth is all *anyone* needs is Jesus and His love, including those of us in ministry. The Lord has used the nursing home ministry to get and keep our minds right.

However, another immense blessing is that the Holy Spirit love, joy, peace, gentleness, and wisdom that the Lord pours to us and through us in the care facilities refuses to *stay* in the care facilities. They are truly *following us* all the days of our lives, and they show up in a mighty way on Sunday mornings as well. We have never experienced more Holy Spirit love, joy, and peace on Sunday mornings as we do now. I have no doubt part of the reason is the Lord rewarding us for being obedient and following Him to His children in the care facilities.

I wanted to grow my ministry;
Jesus wanted to grow my faith, hope, and love.

Just one of the rewards the Lord has brought to our Sunday morning worship is personified in the story of Fred, Marsha, and McKayla. Fred and Marsha had not attended worship for twenty years. They began worshipping with us on Sunday mornings and before too long they were bringing their precious seven-year-old granddaughter, McKayla, along as well. McKayla had a beautiful heart for Jesus from the beginning and instantly became a faithful, joyful attender with her grandparents. They always sat near the front of the worship area. However, one Sunday I noticed that McKayla was no longer sitting with her grandparents. She was now seated by herself in the front row *directly* in front of the worship team. She was focused so intently upon them that the thought occurred to me, *Looks like someone in the band owes McKayla some money!* Next Sunday, the same thing happened, as it did the following Sunday. By the fourth Sunday, she showed up with a homemade "microphone" her grandmother helped her make out of a wire kitchen whisk, aluminum foil, and black and silver ribbon! She began singing along on her microphone. The next week Craig Coffman, our music coordinator, invited her and her special microphone to join the band. However, once Craig actually heard McKayla sing, he gave her a live mike! This is another example of Spirit-led ministry, because little McKayla has an *incredible* voice. The Spirit gave her this gift of music, began moving in her heart and mind to sing, she patiently processed it, made her own microphone, and now she uses her gift to bless us all in worship. She also encouraged her mother, who has a beautiful voice as well. When she is able to attend worship, she joins McKayla and sings in the praise group, too. The Lord works in mysterious and awesome ways!

But what about growing the ministry? Isn't that our most important job? Actually, it is not part of our job *at all*! It is Jesus' job, and He has done and is doing a remarkable job: "And I tell you, you are Peter, and on this rock *I will build my church*, and the gates of hell shall not prevail against it." (Matthew 16:18) Jesus has built His church from a ragtag group of people to over 1.6 billion people today! His job is to build His ministry throughout the world, and He is doing a fine job. Our job is to be faithful followers of Jesus, loving God and others, serving the least, leading by example, and helping others become followers of Jesus as well. Jesus is with us, making His disciples through us. *Refocus.*

One of the results of this revelation is that we no longer do long range planning. The pressure is off. Think about it: how can we *possibly* know what God has in store for His ministry one, two, five, even ten years down the road? Who knows the mind of God and His plans for us? We used to do long range planning all the time. Sometimes we met the goals and felt pride. The vast majority of the time we did not and felt shame. *Neither* feeling is of God! I think we mostly went through this process to make us feel like we were being proactive. Now we literally have no goals other than to be faithful each day, excited to see what the Lord has next for us. If the Lord begins to move in our hearts about what *might* be the next thing He has for us, we pray and discuss the idea. Then we pray some more and discuss some more. If it becomes a goal for us, it is always written in pencil. We have started many ministries. By the time they reach fruition, most look completely different from our original plan. The Hidden Treasures thrift store I mentioned earlier is just one example. We started it for us. God blessed and built it for others.

Remember, Jesus was constantly surprising His disciples. They had no idea what was next. We are no different. Give up control. We are to walk by faith and not by sight. Jesus tells us that we must become like children to see and enter Heaven. The greatest faith is childlike faith; not child*ish* and immature, but childlike! Other than our Heavenly Father, who knows what is coming next? Live the adventure He created you to live. Buckle up with Jesus and hang on!

This scripture was not recently added to the Bible, but somehow I missed it for years. "Look here, you people who say, 'Today or tomorrow we are going to such and such a town, stay there a year, and open up a profitable business.' How do you know what is going to happen tomorrow? For the length of your lives is as uncertain as the morning fog—now you see it; soon it is gone. What you ought to say is, 'If the Lord wants us to, we shall live and do this or that.' As it is, you boast in your arrogant schemes. All such boasting is evil.'" (James 4:13-16)

"If the Lord wants us to" is the way every plan should start, and when something is truly from God and begins to develop—watch out! The Holy Spirit will grow the passion, the unity, and the plan, and everything will simply fall into place. There will be no stopping it.

As we allow the Holy Spirit to take over the entirety of his ministry, including the future, with an understanding that God's ways are not the world's ways, the Lord will honor and bless the ministry. Why does the Bible direct us to widows and orphans? As one lady shared at a recent gathering, "It is because they can't do anything for us." Exactly! If we are actually serving and caring for people who can do nothing for us, then it must be Christ in us doing the work. If it is me, there is always an angle. If it is Jesus, it is selfless, loving service. And if it is Christ in me, it will be pure power!

An often overlooked teaching of Scripture is found in Matthew 11:28-30. In it, Jesus says, "Come to me, all who labor and are heavy laden, and I will give you rest. Take my yoke upon you, and learn from me, for I am gentle and lowly in heart, and you will find rest for your souls. For my yoke is easy, and my burden is light." At first glance, our Lord seems to be simply telling us that when we are tired, stressed, and overwhelmed, that we are to trust Jesus with those burdens. He will then carry them and give us peace and rest. But there is much more than that in these few sentences.

Quite simply, His work done His way is Holy Spirit powered. It is the life I was created to live.

Jesus also discusses His "yoke." Verses 29 and 30 are both about his yoke. A yoke is for *work*—the work that Jesus has for us to do. As long as we are here the Lord has work for us. As we come to Him and follow Him, we will experience relief and regeneration as we serve others by *taking on* His work, connected with Him, learning from Him, and experiencing rest for our souls every step of the way. His work and the burden of serving with Him are described, then, as being easy and light. Why? Who do you think is doing the heavy lifting, you or Jesus? Who has the burden of knowing what work there is to do, you or Jesus? Who knows the perfect, pleasing plan, you or Jesus? When I am submitting to Jesus and working with Him, He leads me into the center of God's will for me. That is where my soul is at rest.

As long as we have breath in our bodies, the Lord has work for us to do with Him. We remind our brothers and sisters in the care facilities of this all the time, and Jesus reminds us right back! We will say to them, "As the staff is caring for you physically, you care for them spiritually. Let them know how thankful you are for them. Ask them how their lives are going. Let them know you are praying for them and that Jesus loves them. Ask them if you can pray for them right now. You may be the one that gets the joy of bringing them home to Jesus!"

The temptation to believe that you don't count, that there is nothing God has for you to do, or that somehow God's work is always great and noticed by the world so, therefore, you must be failing is a *devastating* lie of the enemy. All he does is lie! Don't believe him. At the very least, all of us can all have a prayer list of people we bring every day before our Father. Besides, is there a greater gift of love we can do for others than praying for them? I don't believe so.

Mother Theresa put it this way: "I never concerned myself with doing great things. Only little things with great love." Praise God! To be honest, the world doesn't need great things. The world needs the great love of Jesus pouring out of His humble followers in the little things of life.

The Lord has shown me that when I go my own way and follow my own plans, He refuses to bless me with Holy Spirit power. It is *my* yoke, my plan, and I am doing all the pulling. He will allow me to struggle and complain as long as I want. He also withholds his joy and peace. However, when I repent, rededicate, restructure my life around Jesus daily, and refocus on being yoked with Him as we serve others, the work becomes effortless because Holy Spirit-led ministry is also Holy Spirit-*fed* ministry. Quite simply, His work done His way is Holy Spirit powered. It is the life I was created to live. He will not bless me with pure power until I submit. Then He helps me start becoming the *real* me, as our Father whispers to my soul, "Well done! I am so proud of you." That's the joy of the Lord!

Chapter 8

Blessed are those who hunger and thirst for righteousness,
for they shall be satisfied.
MATTHEW 5:6

O bedience to our Father is rewarded with Holy Spirit joy. The joy of the Lord provides contentment and power regardless of one's circumstances. This is an incredible secret the Apostle Paul learned the hard way. "I know how to be brought low, and I know how to abound. In any and every circumstance, I have learned the secret of facing plenty and hunger, abundance and need. I can do all things through him who strengthens me." (Philippians 4:12-13)

Paul Hoffland has discovered this as well. He coached high school and junior college football for over forty years and was well into his retirement years when I asked to meet with him. The catalyst for my request was a need to know how to best impact the lives of the men in our congregation for Christ. Who better to ask than a successful football coach? I'd noticed that we had many women in Bible study groups, but relatively few men. We had women serving in lots of ways, but relatively few men. I'd even say from the pulpit on Sunday mornings, "Fellas, we're behind the women spiritually. We need to catch up." In effect, I was saying that the men needed to be more like women.

In short order, the Holy Spirit convicted me that I was dead wrong about that, and I even sent out an email to the congregation, saying, "I owe all of you a huge apology. Come this Sunday and hear what it is." That's when I said, "Men, please forgive me. We are not behind women spiritually. But we do have a different spirituality. I promise to pray and seek God's will so that all of us, whether men or women, will grow closer to Jesus." The problem was that I didn't know how to speak to that different spirituality.

So Paul came and took a seat in my office. Even in retirement, he still looked the part; if I had the wardrobe available, I could've had him change into a t-shirt, shorts, and wear a coach's whistle and I would've been ready to drop to the floor and give him twenty. It's probably why he's known around Light of Christ as "Coach Paul." I asked him to tell me his story of being a coach. "You must know something about reaching and motivating young men," I said. "I want to learn. What is the key?"

"High expectations," he answered. "I told the boys each year that there are no stars on this team. We are all going to give our best, starting with me as the head coach. If we will play for each other and give our best for the team, and not worry about personal glory, we're going to be hard to beat." He talked about how he went into many inner-city homes, sat with the young athlete who may never have had a father figure in his life, and told him that he expected him to come into the football program and be a leader.

A light flashed on in my mind. High expectations.

"How many young men do you think you coached over the years, Paul?"

"Maybe three thousand."

"How many quit the team because your expectations were too high?" I asked.

"Three."

That's it! The reason we have so few men in church and involved in ministry is not because our expectations are too high; it's because they are insultingly, pathetically low! We are not challenging them with the vision that God has for them. Then I thought about how Jesus' first disciples were just ordinary guys who responded over time to the great calling He modeled before them in how He lived His life and in how He served others. It wasn't the miracles that drew these men. It was *Jesus Himself!*

When others turned their back and refused to follow Christ (John 6:66), this core remnant of men stuck around—and all they did was walk with Jesus, learn from Jesus, and help each other stay faithful. It was so simple.

From that day onward, I asked Coach Paul to pray with me about what God wanted to do for the men of Light of Christ. I didn't ask Paul to start a men's ministry; I didn't ask him to do anything except pray—and we did over the next nine months, meeting once a week to share any insights God had given us. At the close of that nine month period, Coach Paul responded to the call of God and came out of "retirement" to lead our men. "I had been retired for thirteen years and playing a lot of golf," Paul said. "It was at that point where I felt life was too short, and I needed to do something more with my retirement. My heart has been filled with joy as I've worked with these men."

"Why are you being so nice to me?"

The men's ministry has three goals: to make spiritual leaders of the men for their families, to use the Bible as their playbook, and to grow spiritually. It started with a breakfast of about forty men and five small Bible study groups and has burgeoned to no less than seventeen Bible study teams and other outreach events. "In my email communications to the men," Paul says, "I greet everyone using the word, 'Gentlemen.' This ministry has placed a gentler spirit in our men. They are more relaxed and comfortable with their lives. It has changed the way they think and act. We concentrate on being the very best men we can for the people that we serve."

Part of this gentle spirit is shown in how the men are more com-mitted to our Heavenly Father and in how they consistently bring their families to our Father's House for worship. The men bring their families out of love for God and the realization that we owe the Lord absolutely everything. After all He has done for us, if we cannot commit two hours on Sunday to worship, praise, and thank Him, and bring our families to Him so they can learn to love Him as well, then we are off track. So many women have asked me, "What are you doing to my husband? He's totally changing!" I respond, "We're not doing anything; it's all the Holy Spirit." After one man attended only *two* bible discussions, the change in him was so dramatic that his wife told me later she actually began crying and asked him, "Why are you being so nice to me?"

We listen to Jesus, He changes us, and it is always for the better. He also adds wonderful rest and peace to our souls. Our men are moving forward in their unique spirituality not to be like the ladies (we make lousy women anyway) but to thrive as men of God, cherishing the high expectations the Lord has for them—and that they now have for themselves.

One of the really amazing aspects to our Bible discussion groups is how everyone encourages me! They want to listen and follow Jesus. They want to become the men and women God created them to be. They are not distracted with the *business* of ministry. It is simply about Jesus and how He leads us every day. Their focus helps my focus. One day I confessed to a group of men, "You know, guys, I am so sorry. I am a pastor. I get paid to stay close to Jesus, and I have failed miserably. It is my job to listen and follow Him, but I'm afraid I haven't done a very good job." A dear brother in Christ looked at me and simply said, "It is all of our jobs." Thank you, Lord Jesus, for your grace pouring through them to me.

Today, Rod Moran and his son Kyle are greeters on Sunday morning, welcoming people as they arrive for service. This is quite remarkable given that Rod says he used to hate people. "You leave me alone and I will leave you alone," was his unspoken mantra. However, he was faithful in bringing his family to worship.

From time to time I sensed the Spirit encouraging me to invite Rod to join one of our men's groups. He would politely listen to my invitations, but would later say to his wife, "I'm not joining those freaks." However, the Lord did not give up on him. The Holy Spirit gave another men's group member, Bob Grochowski, a heart for Rod. Bob and Rod are both men's men, defensive linemen sized fellas who take no prisoners and ask no questions. Bob kept praying for Rod and would also consistently invite him to our Saturday morning men's Bible discussion. Finally, Rod agreed to join us. In that session we talked about Malachi 3:10 and its message to give the first ten percent of everything we have to the Lord as a tithe. Rod listened in as one of the guys asked an unusual question.

"So what if a pimp starts coming to church," he conjectured. "He wants to give an offering, and we know where that money has come from. Do we take it and present it to God?"

Everybody started looking around, and several heads turned in my direction. "Hey, guys, I don't know the answer," I said. "What do you think?

After some further discussion, one of the other men asked, "Well, is he a *tithing* pimp?" We laughed so hard I thought some guys were going to pass out. Rod later said that he knew at that moment he was going to fit in perfectly with the group. Before we returned to the Word, the consensus in the group was that we would probably take the offering and then donate it to the Dream Center, which also helps rescue girls out of prostitution.

The point is there was no veneer or façade of holiness. The group was a collection of ordinary guys who acknowledge Jesus as the extraordinary one—and the Lord used that safe setting, where we listened to Jesus and helped each other, to chip away at Rod's bubble of hate and safety until it shattered into a tireless love for others.

"Most people have a three-foot personal space," Rod said, "but I had a sixty-foot bubble. I didn't want to know anybody, and I didn't want them to know me. That was broke down quite a bit by coming to Light of Christ. We moved down here with no family or friends, and we got to know friends who turned into family—and we needed that family when our oldest daughter was killed in a car accident eight years ago."

"That's when God really took hold of my life," he said, "because I had anger issues. He tore all of that down, and this Light of Christ family just stepped up in miraculous ways just to help us out through that time. I am so thankful to God for that."

"This church is such a family," said Rod's wife, Linda. "I don't even know how to describe this church, but they care so much about everybody. People who have been here forever, people that have left, people who have come back, or are coming for the first time—everything goes back to Jesus. It's just like Rod said. When we lost our daughter from the car accident, there were so many loving arms around us, and prayers that you felt."

Rod and Linda's beautiful daughter, Cara, was killed by a drunk driver on a Saturday night as she and her friends were driving back to their college. Rod and Linda were contacted early Sunday morning, called me, and I went to be with them before the Sunday service began. Before I left for worship, I assured them we were going to pray for their family and that I'd return as soon as possible.

We prayed for the entire family at the beginning of worship. I asked everyone to remember the Moran family in prayer as often as possible. There were a lot of tears. After we finished putting everything away following the worship service, I hurried back to their house. It was difficult to find parking! Their home was packed. At least twenty people from the congregation felt led by the Holy Spirit to go to them. I was astonished. I shouldn't have been. Although I had not asked anyone to go to them, Jesus did. He spoke to His people and they followed Him to Rod and Linda's home, letting them know they were not alone. He gave us His heart for them. This is all Jesus, and He gets all the glory!

Rod believes God prepared them for what was going to happen to their daughter by bringing them to Light of Christ. "I don't believe our family would be together right now had it not been for His love and support, and the support and love from the Light of Christ family." Thankfully, Rod had been in his men's Bible discussion group for a few years prior to Cara's death. He fell back on his biblical training as he immediately reached up to our Heavenly Father. Astonishingly, Rod said he never had an ounce of hatred for the drunk driver. This from a man who says he used to hate everybody? *Only* Jesus can do that!

The amazing work of the love of God in Rod's life is never more apparent than when he and Kyle greet folks every Sunday morning as they arrive for church. "Ten, fifteen years ago, there's no way that's me,"

Rod said. "I wanted to be the guy sitting in the back of the church, not knowing anyone. Now, to know I'm standing at the door, handing out bulletins, and people say 'Oh, this is so wonderful you're doing this?' Actually, I consider it my blessing. I get to see all of the smiles as people come through the door, and get the hugs, handshakes, and high fives. My heart has been softened for broken and hurting people. He's working through me so that people see a smile and a kind hand…which is all through Him. I have nothing to do with it."

⁜

Almost every ministry wants to figure out how to get men like Rod into the Bible, as men learn how to listen to Jesus and grow in their faith. Wonderful! Here are some things many congregations have tried:

- Sunday morning class with the pastor teaching
- Men's groups that follow a study guide
- Couples groups that follow a study guide
- A monthly men's breakfast with a guest speaker
- Nothing at all, because there is no way ordinary guys will ever want to read and discuss the Bible!

If you are doing any of these things and they are working for you, great! Keep doing what you're doing. However, none of them worked for us. This surprised me—particularly the couples groups. I thought the men would come because their wives made them. Some did, and the truth is, we do have one very strong couples group at Light of Christ. For most of our families, though, a couples group did not work for a variety of reasons, not the least of which being providing child care.

But I also think there are two hidden reasons why couples groups tend to struggle. First, our experience was that when men and women are in a group, the women tended to do most of the talking. Men often focused on being the comic relief in the group. The problem with this is men are not comics. Our Father wants us to become the men of God He created us to be. Genuine sharing from everyone is critically important in becoming disciples, but oftentimes the men will clam up when they are in a group with women. Second, men and women are different. Get a group of men together and have them pick out a movie to go see—and then do the same with a group of women. It is an absolute guarantee they will choose different movies. In the same way, we have different *spiritualities*. We approach things from different perspectives—and that is a good thing! More than that, it is a very good thing. Our experience is that when men are with men and women are with women, everyone is then able to share and communicate at a much deeper level.

So should we give up on couples groups? Absolutely not! Simply pray about it. It may be that the Lord leads you to tweak your group a bit. For example, in our midweek meeting, everyone begins together as we share prayer concerns and read the primary scripture. Then we divide into men's and women's groups for discussion. *The optimum size of each group is four to six participants.* Each group looks at the Bible passage and discusses what they see. Then, after about a half hour, all of us come back together and share our insights. It's incredible! And the laughter? One of our guys told me, "I haven't laughed this much since college when I would go to parties and get drunk. This is so much better. Plus, there is never a hangover with Jesus!"

We are helping each other do
the only necessary thing: listen to Jesus.
The Holy Spirit ignites and grows our faith.

In addition, we *only* use the Word of God. It is the sword of the Spirit. Watch and see how the Spirit is unleashed in these groups—drawing brothers and sisters in Christ closer than ever before, speaking to us as only He can, and teaching each one of us precisely what we need to know—when only the Bible is discussed in an environment of gentleness, encouragement, love, and joy. We are helping each other do the only necessary thing: listen to Jesus and faith is ignited! A conservative estimate is that ninety-five percent of everyone who has remained in these Bible discussion groups at Light of Christ has experienced incredible, miraculous life transformation. We currently have over sixty-three percent of our men in weekly bible discussion groups, and the percentage continues to grow. All glory to God!

Plus, this is not just for the adults. In our Sunday morning services, we all worship together for the first half hour, and then the children and youth are dismissed from the worship area for their Sunday school time. Our youth do the same thing as the adults: take a scripture, read it, and then our leaders ask them, "What do you see? What caught your eye?" The Holy Spirit takes it from there! However, children and youth are welcome to stay in worship with their parents if they would like. One family attended Light of Christ for a few weeks, and I noticed that their teenage son remained with them in worship. I thought it was because he loved listening to me—but actually his mom had encouraged him to go to the high school group because he was falling asleep during my sermons. (*It seems the Lord never misses an opportunity to teach me humility!*) This young man resisted for awhile, but he finally relented and went with the other youth. After worship and Sunday school concluded, his mom asked him, "Well, did you enjoy it?" He answered, "Mom, it was amazing! They actually want to know what I think!"

Every couple of months, the church's youth team has a fellowship time for the youth during Sunday school where all of the youth from fifth through twelfth grades gather together for fellowship and games. Libby Vincent, our coordinator of youth ministry, told me about one time when the leaders forgot to check the fifth and sixth grade classroom. Sure enough, a group of young people were patiently waiting for class to begin. When no youth leader arrived to lead the discussion, one of the students named Jackson took the lead. He had everyone open to one of his favorite Bible verses learned at summer camp, Romans 16:19-20. They read the verses and then discussed what it meant to each of them. They spent the entire class time sharing what those verses meant to them, and all without an adult leader! Praise be to God.

If you wonder if this will work in your setting, there is a brother in

Christ in the Seattle area who visited us and wanted to learn about men's ministry. We shared with him what the Lord has shown us. However, he took it a step further. He began a men's Bible discussion group in his *neighborhood*. He now has six men meeting with him every week to listen to Jesus, discuss His life and teaching, and help each other. Three of them don't even attend church, but they will not miss their men's group! Ordinary men are not excited listening to a lecture about Jesus, or having to come up with a particular answer to a study guide's question, but they love listening *to* Jesus. Even if they don't know Him yet.

Here is the information we gave him to facilitate his group. I believe this format will work in any setting:

Take quality time every day to be in the Word yourself. Learn to listen to Jesus and our Heavenly Father. The more you listen to Him, the more excited you will be to help others learn how to listen to Him. As the old saying goes, passionate faith is caught not taught! Focus on Jesus; His words and His life. Matthew, Mark, Luke, or John is the best place to start with this type of Bible discussion.

Your primary role is to facilitate discussion. Remind your group there is no right or wrong answers; we are simply discussing what we see. Thank them for their responses. Allow the discussion to move where the Spirit leads it, realizing He will do the teaching. From time to time you will need to help the focus return to the Word. You know what is better than teaching others? Patiently encouraging them to wrestle with the text, share what they see, and watch the Spirit ignite their faith!

Remember, you are providing a safe place for people. They enter believing whatever they believe. That is fine. Jesus took people right where they were. Ordinary people loved listening to Him, and the more they listened, the more He began to change them. Same dynamic here: the Holy Spirit is big enough to bring people home. Be patient with them. Be patient with yourself. Be patient with the Spirit. See what the Lord does.

1. Have everyone sit in a circle. If there is anyone new (or relatively new), have everyone share first names.

2. Fellowship time: how is everyone's week going? (ten minutes)

3. Prayer: ask the Lord to open our eyes and hearts to the leading of the Spirit. Thank Him for being with the group and everyone in the group. Ask Him to bless those who couldn't attend.

4. Read only five-six verses. Go around the circle, each person reading one verse, until the section is covered. Then ask, "What do you see?" or "What jumps out at you?" or "What catches your eye?"

5. Patiently wait for their responses. Be comfortable with silence. You probably have something you see and would like to share, but please understand: your most important role is not sharing but drawing out other people's responses. Once people have shared their thoughts feel free to share yours.

6. Possible responses after fifteen seconds (or so) of quiet:
   - "Don't everybody talk at once." Sometimes you can simply say, "Bueller. Bueller." And that is enough to break the ice, get people laughing and sharing.
   - Sometimes the passage is difficult. Admit it! "You know what, this is a tough passage. I'm not seeing a lot yet either, but let's keep looking. The Spirit will show us what He wants us to see."
   - If there is a particular verse that catches your eye, guide the group to that verse like this: "Take a look at verse sixteen. What do you see there?" After others have shared, feel free to share why it spoke to you. *General rule: they share first, you share last.*

- After patiently wrestling with those verses, and once you feel the Spirit moving you on, consider the next five to six verses and repeat this process. It could be those initial verses fill up the entire time. We like to keep our groups right at one hour: ten minutes fellowship, forty minutes discussion, ten minutes wrap-up and closing prayer.

7. End the Bible discussion time with about ten minutes left. Thank everyone for participating and that what they have shared has been a blessing. Remind them that if they have a desire to invite a friend, that's probably Spirit led. Inviting is our responsibility; getting them there is the Spirit's. Just obey.

8. Closing prayer: invite everyone to lift up someone else. Generally speaking, people are open to praying for someone else if everyone else is as well. With a new group, you may want to pray the closing prayer yourself. Since you are modeling prayer for people, short and simple prayers are best.

There is unbelievable power in the Word of God. It is easy to forget here in America, where many Bibles haven't been taken down from shelves in years.

> Our problem is not that Bibles are illegal or hard
> to come by or dangerous to give to others.
> Our problem is we don't know the power of
> God unleashed through His Word!

Let me share with you another story our "Brother John" from the Middle East told us at the Voice of the Martyrs conference. Three young followers of Jesus, each around twenty years of age, decided they wanted to get Bibles into the hands of as many Muslims as possible. Their idea was to go to the mosque on Friday, the Muslim holy day. They waited until the end of the service and then, as people were leaving the mosque, they gave each of them a New Testament and encouraged them to read about Jesus.

The men receiving the New Testaments were at first curious, but then some started to become agitated, and then angry. The three young men now felt it would be best to leave, especially since they saw the Imams (Muslim religious leaders) making their way through the crowd to see what was going on. However, they were surrounded with no path of escape. The head Imam demanded to know what they were doing. One of the young men spoke up and told him they were simply handing out holy books and inviting people to read them. The Imam took one and slowly began paging through it, taking time to read different sections. This went on for fifteen minutes—and the young men realized their earthly lives hung in the balance. When the Imam finished, he took the New Testament, kissed it, held it to his forehead, and then raising it into the air, said, "Everyone gets one of these today!"

The Word of God will speak to the heart of every man, woman and child. Our problem is not that Bibles are illegal or hard to come by or dangerous to give to others. Our problem is we don't know the power of God unleashed through His Word! Our men are living and breathing examples of what the Spirit can do in our lives when we allow people a safe place to read about Jesus and his teaching, share our thoughts, and watch the Lord speak to us all.

As we listen to Jesus He turns us into servants who follow the Great Servant.

Chapter 9

When they had finished breakfast, Jesus said
to Simon Peter, "Simon, son of John, do you love me
more than these?" He said to him, "Yes, Lord; you know
that I love you." He said to him, "Feed my lambs."
JOHN 21:15

E ach year, our men's ministry under Coach Paul's leadership performs two major outreaches, one internal and the other external. They host and cook a Mother's Day brunch that the women of our church appreciate and return for year after year, and they conduct a golf tournament fundraiser to benefit Feed My Starving Children (FMSC). Light of Christ first learned about FMSC from a young couple in our congregation, Alan and Jamie Dean. They had visited FMSC with friends from another church, and insisted that we needed to take a group to FMSC to volunteer in packing food boxes. I thought it was a great idea and decided to join the forty or so folks who went that first time in 2010.

FMSC had a temporary office at that time located in nearby Tempe, AZ, and as a group we worked for two hours. At the end of our session, we were shown a video about the children our packages were going to feed—and our hearts were captured. Clearly, these were not just hungry children, as tragic as that is; these were indeed starving children that, without our help that day, would surely die. One story was of an emaciated child found living in a Port-o-Potty. Within three months he had been nourished back to a healthy state, and the photo of him three years after that was just beautiful, his smile glowing across his face.

Over the next several months, we returned time and again, and I even lobbied the national offices of FMSC to make sure the Phoenix area was given a permanent facility for this dynamic ministry. Our men's ministry launched the annual golf tournament to help FMSC. As of today, our tournament has raised over $70 thousand for the organization, and our congregation has given at least another $40 thousand on top of that. The great news is that the national organization not only decided to put a permanent site here in the Valley of the Sun, but it is now the largest FMSC packing site in the entire country! Thank you, Father.

Let's be clear: as much as the starving children of the world need the food provided by FMSC, our spiritually starving children here in America need to be involved in something that *actually* makes a difference in the lives of others. Our children are drowning in an ocean of entertainment, self-centeredness, and stimuli. Even within Christian ministries our kids are blasted with entertainment to the point of overload, when they should simply be given every possible chance to join in the great adventure of listening to Jesus and following Him as we work with Him to care for others in need. Our teenagers have invited other teenage friends to join them in our monthly gatherings at FMSC, and some kids have even decided to have their birthday parties there after seeing the amazing work achieved by this ministry. We are not created to sit in front of a video game console; we are created to get outside of ourselves, follow Jesus and care for other people.

Janine Skinner, the Feed My Starving Children development advisor for the Mesa, AZ office, says one of the unique aspects of volunteering with FMSC is that anyone in the family can participate, starting with children as young as five years of age. "On the one end, you're trying to instill a love of service in your young children and show them that they can give back, and that they are blessed and are therefore called by God to make the world a better place. On the flip side, you've got folks in their older years that also need to have that opportunity to see that they are still useful and can still make a difference."

Everyone in the family makes an impact, she said, and they learn throughout the course of a two-hour visit. "There's an educational piece, there is the actual doing of the packing which is really fun and energetic, and at the end there is a wrap-up session where you find out how many meals were packed, how many kids will be fed, and you can even try the food," she said. "That's where we see the transformation. People come in for the first time and they are blown away about the difference they can personally make in just a short amount of time."

Skinner points out that FMSC has a delivery success rate of 99.7 percent to some of toughest, more hunger-prone areas in the world. "We're working with people who work in-country and know what they're doing there. It's exciting for people to know that when they pack these meals, they're going to get there; they're not stuck in transit or in some corrupt government leaders' hands. They're doing what they're supposed to do," she said, adding that she believes prayer plays a vital role in that success rate. "At the end of each packing session, we pray over the meals that we've just packed; when a shipping container has been filled for delivery to the shipping port in Los Angeles, we go and pray over each one."

However, FMSC also had to go through a time of repenting, rededicating, restructuring, and refocusing before they could rejoice as they are now. Janine continues, "FMSC has always been a Christian organization, but we set God to the side in the early days in an attempt to be more accessible to our corporate volunteers and donors. From 1987 to 2003, we packed a total of 26 million meals and our growth each year was minimal while the need around the world increased. In 2003, our Board of Directors made the decision to rededicate FMSC to Christ, putting the Lord front and center in all that we do and in every decision that we make."

What happened next? "Our growth and our health as an organization since then has been phenomenal! We've packed and shipped more than 1.2 *billion* meals and we've grown an average of forty-six percent year-over-year since 2003. There is no way this could have happened without God at the helm," she said. "Our ability to maintain this growth is completely in God's hands. As our reach increases and our staff grows, we seek God's guidance in all that we do, knowing that His plan for FMSC is always so much bigger and better than our own and that He delights in our work together to feed His kids!"

No one doubts our Lord wants us to feed His children throughout the world. However, it seems our Heavenly Father was patiently waiting for FMSC to repent of setting Him to the side, rededicate the ministry to Jesus, restructure their ministry around daily prayer and submission to Him, continue focusing on caring for His starving children, and then rejoicing as the Holy Spirit has been unleashed, feeding more children than they ever could have imagined. And He has chosen them to be part of it!

Praise God for His pure power. Spirit-led ministry is about doing God's ministry in God's way. It also involves the Lord bringing us to other Spirit-led ministries we can joyfully support so they can serve even more. We are immensely blessed at Light of Christ to be a very, very small part of what God is doing through Feed My Starving Children!

Before he was back in his seat she
was at the table, wrote down a higher bid, and added
something new—she turned and *glared* at him.

In the second year of our annual golf tournament for FMSC, my then nine-year-old daughter Noelle had her eyes set on one of the prizes up for bid for the event: a football signed by Arizona Cardinals' wide receiver Larry Fitzgerald from their regular season game against the Philadelphia Eagles the previous year. She had already worked it out that she could get the ball in our silent auction, and then sell it later to help put herself through college. The way children's minds work! She was determined to win that ball, no matter what.

Linda and I agreed that Noelle could use her savings to bid on the ball. She went up to the table and wrote down the first bid. She then returned to her seat and focused like a laser on that paper. Pretty soon a gentleman walked up to the table, perused many of the other silent auction items, focused on the Larry Fitzgerald ball, and wrote on that sheet. Noelle was not happy! She reported her displeasure to us and we said, "Well, that's the way this goes. Whoever puts in the highest bid at the end gets the ball. You can't keep people from bidding. Besides, all of the money is going to feed starving children, so the more the football goes for, the better." She was up like a shot, went to the table, wrote down a higher bid, and returned to her seat. No one was going to outbid her!

A few minutes later, the same gentleman walked up to the table, looked at a few other items, returned to the football, and wrote another number. Noelle was almost apoplectic! Before he was back in his seat she was at the table, wrote down a higher bid, and added something new— she turned and *glared* at him. Sure enough, though, the man returned and increased the bid. This happened a couple of more times with Noelle shooting optical fireballs at him from across the room. Linda and I were a bit confused why he kept outbidding her. All we could figure was somehow the football meant a lot to him.

We finally put a stop to it. Noelle's bid was up to six hundred dollars and we told her she could not go any higher. She was not happy about it, but she let it go. Coach Paul then came up to us and said, "Don't leave." Apparently, the man who had been bidding against Noelle was a friend of his.

Once the luncheon was over and people were clearing out of the banquet hall, the gentleman who had won the football came over to our table. Noelle was so upset she refused to even look at him. Coach introduced him. "Noelle, this is my friend, Joel. He wants to tell you something."

With a huge smile on his face, Joel put the ball down in front of her and said, "I got this for you." She didn't know what to do; her face betrayed a million emotions all at once! We made her get up and give him a hug. He told us, "I haven't had that much fun in years! You have quite a little girl there." Later she took a picture with the football, wrote a nice note, and sent them to him. She now has the football proudly displayed in a glass case. Every time I see it, the joyful memory returns.

Noelle decided to donate her six hundred dollars as well so that even more children could be saved. Praise God! Childlike faith, joyful generosity, fun, and even a little frustration that God works out—all as we follow Jesus to care for others. Thank you, Lord!

Our Heavenly Father continued to infuse us with this attitude of service and bring forth even more of the miraculous in our midst. The women's ministry was next on His agenda, and what the Lord has done through our amazing sisters is simply remarkable.

⁜

Before the transformation of our men's ministry, our women's ministry was running along with small groups all using some sort of a study guide. Yet the simpler approach to discussing the Bible used by our men started getting the ladies' attention.

One in particular was Becky Mason, who is now our coordinator of women's ministries. She had originally come to us from another church; she decided to stay because she felt the Lord was drawing her to our congregation because of our focus on listening to Jesus and following Him into the world to serve others. She started attending one of our women's study groups, had experienced for herself the simple power of getting into God's Word, but didn't wish to be the one to direct the group. Going into the meeting that night, Becky had been praying that the women would decide to adopt the Bible discussion format the men were using.

"It's been one of my greatest joys being involved in the discussion groups. We began by using study guides. Our first guide was a good one and a blessing to everyone but we were ready take a new turn and just use the Bible as our only guide," Becky said. "We soon found out that trusting the Holy Spirit to guide us was the very best decision we could have made; now, several years later, there's no going back."

As time went on Becky became involved with our nursing home ministry. "I really was just going to attend one day to help," she insisted. "Well, the folks at the nursing home had my heart that very first day. I'm still going, only now to two facilities every week, and they have become the highlight of my week. As they invite us into their home each week, we are humbled by the sweet, loving way they care for one another. Many times, though their own needs are many, they will request prayers for one of the others."

Becky continued. "My own personal faith has grown so much through the fellowship with my brothers and sisters in Christ and through really giving my time to God and listening to where He wants me to be. It's difficult to describe. My desire is to stay in His will; that's when my joy is overflowing. To be available to go forward and to change as He directs— His ways are always best. My walk with the Lord gets closer all the time, but only when I keep my eyes on Jesus."

The Lord is ready to pour out miracle after miracle on ministries that will repent, rededicate their lives and ministries to Jesus, restructure around listening to Jesus, and then follow the Good Shepherd to care for broken and hurting people. As the miracles of God continue to grow around and within you, the rejoicing kind of happens on its own. We have seen so many "miracle chains" where one miracle leads to another which leads to another. One of my favorite miracle chains, that is still ongoing, began when the Spirit led a humble servant to reach out to her neighbor.

Carolyn Hinrichs was unable to make it to church for years as she cared for her ailing husband, Arnold. Day after day she poured out the love of Jesus to this dear man. After he passed away, she was once again able to attend church regularly. She also began learning what was happening in the lives of others at the retirement community where she lived. One day after service she asked if she could have a word with me.

"Pastor, God has really broken my heart for a lady who just moved into our neighborhood," she said. "She's living with her son now, but she has really gone through a hard time."

I saw the tender concern in Carolyn's eyes. "What is happening in her life?" I asked.

"Well, her name is Joyce, and in just the last two months her husband died, she had a stroke, and she lost her house."

I felt the weight of those burdens and saw the compassion in Carolyn's eyes. "Okay." I paused and then advised, "Just love on her, Carolyn. See what God does as you do."

"I'm eighty-two years old.
Most people think my life is coming to an end."
She shook her head. "My life is just beginning."

A couple of weeks later, Carolyn pulled me aside again, her expression a combination of joy and uncertainty. "I invited Joyce to come to church. I think she's going to come next week."

"That's wonderful, Carolyn!" I said, sensing that a "but" was on its way.

"Yes, it is—but she's Jewish."

"Wow! That'll be great!" I responded, but my mind whispered, *I don't think it's going to happen.*

I was wrong. Next week, there was Carolyn at church with Joyce, a lovely eighty-two year old Jewish woman. I preached my sermon, and afterward Carolyn approached me with her friend. Joyce was crying buckets of tears.

"Pastor, this is Joyce," she said, and in her excitement told me once again, "She's Jewish!"

I smiled. "Praise God! So is Jesus!"

That brought a chuckle to Joyce's weeping. I took her hands. "It looks like God is doing something in your heart today," I told her. She nodded in reply. I continued, "It's all Jesus. He loves you! Just keep coming. What God has begun today, He's going to continue. It's going to be awesome!"

Carolyn returned with Joyce the following week, and once more Joyce was crying, but not as much as before. It was clear that our loving Heavenly Father was working something out inside of her spirit, touching and healing areas of sorrow and hurt. Following Joyce's third Sunday at Light of Christ, Carolyn asked if I could come to her home to visit with the two of them that coming week. We met on Tuesday morning. We had coffee, pastries, and I opened and shared more about the Bible and the Lord. At the end of our time together, Joyce prayed to ask Jesus Christ into her heart as her Savior and Messiah.

The next Sunday was communion, and Joyce was the first one forward, tears in her eyes, to receive the sacrament of her new Lord's body and blood. Later, on the day she was baptized, Joyce told the congregation, "I'm eighty-two years old. Most people think my life is coming to an end." She shook her head. "My life is just beginning."

One Saturday morning we were watching one of our children's soccer games when my phone rang. I noticed it was Joyce. I answered and Joyce asked if I was busy. When she found out we were at the game she told me that she would call later in the day. I assured her I could speak with her right then if she needed. She told me that later would be fine.

However, she did not call that afternoon. I called her but got her voicemail, so I left a message. At worship the next day I asked her, "Joyce, you have been on my mind. Is everything okay?" She told me, "Oh, yes pastor! After hanging up with you I realized I didn't really need to talk with you at all." *Ouch.* She continued, "I just needed to talk with Jesus. So I did, and He told me what to do." Hallelujah!

And wouldn't you know it, the more Joyce talked with Jesus, the more she started serving others. The Lord moved in her heart to begin helping at the nursing home worship services. I recall one lady so feeble that she couldn't clap her hands to the music; Joyce came up behind her, caressed the lady's hands, and helped her to clap to the beat. My eyes sprung a leak. *Lord, isn't this the sweetest thing ever?* I praised God to see a woman who had been through so much to now be able to experience and share the joy of the Lord as He loved others through her!

Chapter 10

I am reminded of your sincere faith, a faith that dwelt
first in your grandmother Lois and your mother Eunice and now,
I am sure, dwells in you as well. For this reason I remind you
to fan into flame the gift of God, which is in you through
the laying on of my hands, for God gave us a spirit
not of fear but of power and love and self-control.
2 TIMOTHY 1:5-7

As Joyce predicted, her story was indeed just beginning. She saved enough money to be able to get her own apartment, and the first thing she wanted to do was host a weekly Bible discussion group. She invited everyone in her apartment complex to attend, and it was set for every Tuesday at 9:00 a.m. She wanted everyone in her apartment complex to know Jesus and His love! The day before the first meeting, Joyce was in the common area of her complex and ran into an old friend she used to see at synagogue. Her name was Nancy. Nancy invited her to an event the next morning.

"I am sorry, but I cannot attend. I already have something planned for tomorrow morning." Joyce replied.

"What is that?" Nancy queried.

Joyce hesitated a second before answering, "I am having a Bible study in my home."

Nancy raised her eyebrows, hesitated as well, and then replied, "I want to come."

Joyce didn't know what to do. She was unsure as to the proper Bible discussion protocol. Instead of saying, "Yes," the first thing out of her mouth was, "I have to check with my pastor first."

She called me that afternoon. "Pastor, my friend Nancy? She's Jewish, and wanted to know if she can come to the Bible study."

It was everything I could do not to bust out laughing. "Absolutely! But first, I want to know something. I just want to make sure I am hearing you correctly. Are you telling me that someone from an entirely different religious background wants to crash your Bible study tomorrow? Is that what you're telling me?"

"Yes, pastor," Joyce said. "Is that *unusual*?"

Then I did laugh. "Yep, just a little bit." I thought to myself, *And here I am trying to get Christians into the Bible. God, you are so at work!*

The next morning, I sat in my car in the parking lot of the complex about ten minutes before it was time to start the study. "Lord, I know you are doing something in Nancy's heart, because this just doesn't happen by itself. Don't let me mess this up." I was anxious because I didn't want to say something trite or be a stumbling block to Nancy.

"Just relax," I sensed the Lord communicating to me. "I'll give you whatever words you need when you need them. Relax."

For one of the few times in my life,
I was truly speechless.
Did I actually just hear what I think I heard?

I took a breath, exited my car, and headed to the apartment. It was me, Joyce, and six other ladies. Joyce pointed out Nancy. She was directly across the coffee table from me, her brown hair pulled back into a tight bun, her face chiseled and stern. We went around the room with introductions and then I began. "We're going to get started in the Gospel of John chapter one, and—"

Nancy's hand shot straight up into the air.

"Yes, Nancy?" I asked.

"Before we start, I have a question." Her tone was decisive.

Lord, help me, I thought. *Here it comes.*

"So. God sent Moses and God sent Jesus. What's the difference?"

A smile came to my face. "Nancy. That's a great question. In fact, it may be *the* question. When we look at all of the people in the Bible, what is the difference between Jesus and all of them? All of us? The Bible says that God didn't just send Jesus—but that He *is* God."

Nancy frowned, tilted her head, sat up straight, raised her eyebrows, and incredulously replied, "You expect me to *believe* that?"

The Lord fulfilled His promise by providing the words precisely when they were needed. "Nancy, I don't expect you to believe anything. We're going to study this one man, Jesus—and you make up your own mind."

Immediately, she smiled. It took all of the edge from her features. "Oh. Okay."

From that day forward, Nancy was the most faithful attendee to the discussions Joyce hosted. With every week, I could see her growing in awareness and faith. The Spirit was doing a mighty, wondrous thing. She often read ahead. "It's all here!" she'd exclaim. "Why didn't the rabbis tell us about Jesus? Everything we need to know is right here!"

One week Nancy shared, "I just tell all of my Jewish friends to pray to Jesus. It's much easier!" Another week she asked, "Is it just me, or is it the more you read about Jesus and His teachings, you just love Him more?" It was delightful!

But I'll never forget the day she delivered this preamble: "I haven't been with a man for over thirteen years."

For one of the few times in my life, I was truly speechless. *Did I actually just hear what I think I heard?* I looked around, and the expressions I saw on the other faces confirmed I had. *I have no idea what's coming next,* I thought, *but I wouldn't miss it for the entire world!* "What did you just say, Nancy?"

"I haven't been with a man for over thirteen years," she repeated, "but now when I go to bed at night, I have my Bible right beside me. If I wake up in the middle of the night and I'm afraid, I reach over and touch my Bible and I know that Jesus is with me and that everything is okay."

Tears immediately filled my eyes as my heart reached out to Jesus. *Lord, help me to fall in love with you and your Word like Nancy has.*

If we as followers of Jesus can learn to simply give people a safe place where they can believe whatever they want and then focus like a laser on Jesus, He is big enough, His words are true enough, and the Holy Spirit is powerful enough to bring them home, in His own time. No manipulation. No program. No coercion. No pressure. Just a safe place where it's okay to ask questions, read about and discuss Jesus, be patient and kind with one another, and watch the Lord work!

At Nancy's baptism, she invited twenty of her Jewish friends to join her on her big day. They all came to the worship service. When it was time for Nancy to come forward, not only did her sponsors from Light of Christ come up on stage with her but, completely on their own and without being asked, so did ten of her Jewish friends—including her sister and brother-in-law! You cannot make this stuff up! There was Nancy, proclaiming her love for Jesus as she was baptized into the faith, surrounded and supported by her Jewish family and friends.

Nancy thanked her Light of Christ family for opening our doors to her. I sensed the Lord immediately changing the sermon for that day. During the sermon I said, "Actually, when you think about it, Jesus was Jewish. All of the first disciples who took the Gospel to the ends of the Earth were Jewish. They gave their lives so we might be saved. All of us Gentiles should thank you, our Jewish brothers and sisters, for loving us enough to bring Jesus to us. We may have opened the church doors to you, but the Lord used you to open Heaven for us. Thank you!" Not long after the baptism Nancy's sister told her, "I love Jesus now, too!"

Today, she calls herself "Nancy, the wandering Jew," drawn to Jesus and His love by Joyce, a Jewish widow, in a loving process started by Carolyn, another widow. All are shining lights for Christ at Light of Christ. Thank you, Father, for this beautiful miracle chain. But it didn't stop there.

One day, the service at the care facility was underway for a few minutes. After singing some powerful songs and sharing some laughter, I felt led to share a story about Nancy. I told about how, after many of Nancy's friends had asked her, "So now you're Christian?" she would respond, "No. I'm still Jewish. Jesus is Jewish! I just love Him with all of my heart. He is my Savior."

As I told the story, a lady I did not recognize spoke up. "That's right! Jesus is Jewish. What a wonderful answer. I never thought of that." Then one of our volunteers, said, "Pastor, that's Sedra. This is the first time she has joined us in worship. She is Jewish."

Then I knew why the Spirit had brought that specific story to mind. It was the perfect one to make Sedra feel at home. I went over to her and kneeled down so I could look into her tear-filled eyes. She said, "I didn't know if it was okay for me to be here."

"Oh, Sedra," I said. "I am so glad you decided to come."

"Me, too," she responded.

We then continued on, and the message I prepared for that day (I no longer preach at any of our three worship services. Lay people bring the Word instead) was about giving your life to Jesus. We prayed, sang a closing song, and then I went back to Sedra. I took her hands in mine and said, "Sedra, thank you so much for joining us in worship."

Her eyes were still filled with tears, but now one of the most beautiful smiles I have ever seen was on her face. She simply said, "I don't know if I have ever been this happy."

"That's Jesus, Sedra," I told her. "That joy is what He brings to all of us. Just talk with Him. Ask for His help every day. He loves you, Sedra. He loves you so very much."

She nodded her head and I had the privilege of giving her a hug.

We never saw Sedra again. Did she ask Jesus into her heart? I believe so, but only the Lord knows for sure. All I do know is what an immense honor it is to be chosen by Almighty God to let these precious and sometimes forgotten people know how much they are truly loved and how much they truly matter. We now have people from the Jewish, Hindu and Muslim faiths as regular participants in our Jesus-focused worship services in the nursing homes. This would have been beyond our belief a few years ago. Nothing is impossible with God!

✛

About a year after she started studying with us, Nancy moved to another apartment complex, this one a care facility for retirees, and started her own Bible discussion group there. True to her nickname, she went door-to-door inviting others to attend. A few didn't like Nancy's direct approach, but it didn't faze her.

The first meeting featured ten kind folks, all Christians from a variety of denominational backgrounds. Then, at the second meeting, we were joined by a group of young men and women, all in purple uniforms and definitely not retiree age. Turns out they were nursing students from Grand Canyon University, a Christian college in Phoenix, who wanted to participate with us. None of them had experienced a discussion group like ours before. One day, we were discussing the first Beatitude from Jesus' Sermon on the Mount. I read, "Blessed are the poor in spirit, for theirs is the kingdom of heaven." (Matthew 5:3)

After a few seconds of looking at the passage, one of the students spoke up. "Pastor, that isn't right. It must be written wrong. It should be 'blessed are the *rich* in spirit.'" She reasoned that a person needed to be rich in spiritual knowledge and awareness.

"That could be true," I said, "but that's not what Jesus said. He said 'poor in spirit.'"

"Well," she countered politely, "maybe what Jesus means is that we are blessed when we *care* for those poor in spirit."

"That's true," I said. "We are blessed when we care for the least, but that's still not what it says. Keep wrestling with it," I encouraged her. "The Holy Spirit will show you."

She let out a tiny huff. "You know the answer, don't you?"

I grinned. "Well, I have an idea—but what is the Bible saying to you? What do you see?"

After a bit more conversation, one of the other students said, "Maybe what Jesus is saying is that when we are at the end of ourselves, when we've tried everything and everyone else, when we are devastated in our spirit and we finally call out to Him—then He gives us the kingdom of Heaven; everything we have ever needed." All glory to God!

Again—a safe place where we listen to Jesus and are patient and gentle with each other.

Anthony and Jenn Jaurigue discovered that sense of safety when the Lord led them to Light of Christ after years of attending church, first in Catholic parishes and then other Protestant churches, and always feeling as though they didn't belong. Their apprehensions weren't helped by Jenn's anxiety disorder, a condition that not only caused panic attacks but at one point kept her confined inside her house for an entire year because she was too afraid to even go outside. Her panic attacks started manifesting themselves right before she and Anthony got married. "I was young and I had no idea, so I went to a doctor and told him, 'I'm dying!' and they were like, 'You're having a panic attack.' I said, 'What's that?' I had no clue."

As they started going to other churches, Jenn experienced anxiety about how her makeup was worn or what she was wearing because of negative comments or perceived attitudes from other churchgoers. Still, they tried their best to fit in—but it wasn't until two friends told them about Light of Christ's preschool and how it could benefit their daughter that they decided to give the church a try. "We felt pushed out of our last church and we were like, 'Do we really want to do all of this again?'" said Jenn. "We were worn down."

Eventually, a full two years after their daughter had attended preschool at Light of Christ, the family came to worship—and have never left. They said everybody was nice and genuine, a marked difference from their earlier church experiences. "At the old place that we had been going to, the pastor we had known for a long time and had helped out in many events had never even bothered to learn our names. Not once."

"The second we walked in," said Anthony of their first visit to Light of Christ, "it was just a different vibe. They introduced themselves; just introduced, like there was no pressure. It was calming, actually. It's a calm you don't even realize is there." Jenn added of later visits, "People asked, 'Oh, we haven't seen you for awhile,' and called us by our names. Just something that simple; we'd never had that happen before."

But that wasn't all God did for the Jaurigue family. They both started attending Bible discussion groups and the Lord used the love of the people and power of His Word and Holy Spirit to take away Jenn's anxiety. "That Bible discussion really saved me," she said, adding that she's now medication free. "And it's just so funny to me because I really have a feel for other people that are just coming in, and I see their eyes are opened, and the Bible becomes a living Bible."

For Anthony, he had lost his youngest brother to cancer and was angry at the Lord for many years. "I didn't understand why. I was just angry and I would always ask, 'Why?' For the longest time I had that on my shoulders," he said. "I started to open up to Pastor Moe and told him about it and our Bible study group talked about it. The actual talking about it and understanding Jesus, understanding how the Lord worked—I felt like a ton of weight just lifted off my shoulders. It was a calming peace because I was talking to people that understood me and didn't judge me. They just wanted to comfort me."

The Holy Spirit transformation in Anthony and Jenn brings a smile to my face every time they come to my mind. They are faithful in worship, Bible discussion groups, and serving others like never before. Their children love coming to both Sunday school and midweek ministries, and are absolutely awesome when we pack food at FMSC! Anthony is an architect. He designed and helped build the stage in our new building. And Jenn, miraculously set free from the anxiety that used to devastate her spirit, is now on staff at Light of Christ. She also volunteers at our Friday worship service at the Chandler Healthcare care facility.

The fruit of the Spirit is our Father's reward when ministries will repent, rededicate, restructure, and refocus. When people, particularly hurting people, visit a Holy Spirit blessed ministry, they simply know something is different. And that difference makes all the difference. They sense the Holy Spirit's love, power, joy, peace, and gentleness. We all do. Thank you, Heavenly Father!

Chapter 11

"Don't I have the right to do what I want
with my own money?
Or are you envious because I am generous?"
MATTHEW 20:15

"Okay," you may be saying to yourself. "This is all well and good. But what about the business aspect of ministry—particularly the issue of funding? Where does being Spirit-led and servant-focused fit in there?"

It was in 2009 that we decided at Light of Christ to leave our mainline denomination. It was out of a strong sense that denominationalism was getting more worldly and less biblical. Essentially, the more biblical a group is (submitting to the Word of God as the final authority), the less political it will be (where the stance or individual that gets the most votes wins). As mainline denominations, or congregations for that matter, move away from the authority of the Word of God, what remains is political infighting no different than what we see every day in Washington, D.C. We just didn't fit any longer within denominationalism, so we blessed those who remained in the denomination, thanked God for them, and transitioned to the new partnerships the Holy Spirit prepared for us.

For seventeen years, the Dingmans prayed for
a place where they could care for homeless children.

All of this time since our first worship service in September 1996, Light of Christ met at one school campus or the other, always grateful but always desiring to find the right property upon which we could build our own facility. As God worked in my life to make Light of Church *His* church, not mine, I strived to pursue building options that I thought were in His plan and will for the church. We owned a piece of property located between two schools in a growing area of Chandler, but when we discovered it was going to cost some $3.2 million there to build twelve thousand square feet, I knew that even if we had the money to do that, it would be downright sinful to spend that much.

So we decided to sell the land. However, the property had a zoning requirement that only a church could be built there. We shopped it to every denomination we could think of, and even proposed mergers with other churches to share the costs and the resources. We made inquiries to the Church of Jesus Christ of Latter-day Saints. Nobody wanted it. Nothing was happening! We knew we couldn't build on it and, apparently, no one was going to buy it. We were stuck with a property that was essentially useless to us and worthless to everyone else.

I was trying to be patient with the Lord. I was striving to keep my ego in check. But I was frustrated and let God know about it. "Well, what's the point, Lord? I don't even know what is happening here," I pled. "Lord, it's your ministry, but I don't see any way out."

Still, we kept moving forward in our desire to listen to Jesus and to serve others. As we continued volunteering and giving to Feed My Starving Children, I heard the Holy Spirit challenge me, "You're helping orphans in other parts of the world through Feed My Starving Children, and that's great. But what about orphans here?" I responded by doing some investigating of local options and discovered Sunshine Acres Children's Home in Mesa. Carol Whitworth, President and CEO of Sunshine Acres, is the daughter of the founders Rev. James and Vera Dingman. As I read about the ministry, I was blown away.

For seventeen years, the Dingmans prayed for a place where they could care for homeless children. Seventeen years! The answer to their prayers came in 1953 when they sold their home, and with the help of the Mesa Optimist Club, made a down payment on 125 acres of Arizona desert with a few rundown buildings. The next year, they opened. Today, Sunshine Acres has cared for almost two thousand children, does not receive government support, and though it is donor funded, they do zero fundraising or solicitation. Friends, businesses, churches, and volunteers contribute and host fundraising events on behalf of the home. Over sixty years ago, Vera Dingman wrote this: "God impressed upon us very strongly that this was His work. We were to take care of the children, and He would take care of the finances."

I was hosted by Carol as I took a tour of their astonishing campus, saw the children they were helping, and felt Holy Spirit conviction that Light of Christ was going to help them. But, oddly enough, I found myself getting angry—at the fact that no one had ever shared this principle with me, or that if they had, I had been too arrogant to listen and learn. *Father, you made this deal with Jim and Vera Dingman. They'll take care of the children, and you'll take care of the finances. Why don't you make that deal with every ministry? And if you do, why hasn't anyone ever told me about this?* I mused. *There is no way it can be this simple!*

Then Carol told me a story that pierced my heart and challenged me to consider that perhaps my understanding of how the Holy Spirit works needed a complete overhaul. It was from forty years earlier when she was serving as the organization's treasurer. It was during a hot, dry August, and the payment on the electric bill was overdue. Power company officials knew her plight, but said they'd done all they could do. If they didn't receive payment by the end of the week, they'd have no other choice but to turn off the power. She took the situation to her father.

"How much do we need?" he asked.

"Two thousand dollars and we have nothing."

He instructed her, "Go ahead and write the check for that amount, put it in the envelope, but don't mail it yet."

So she did as he asked. Later that same day she received a phone call. It was from a law firm. "Sunshine Acres," he said, "has been named a recipient in a settlement that just came through. We're going to have a courier bring the check out to you before the end of the day."

Carol was thankful, surprised, and curious. "Could you tell me how much the check is for?"

He answered, "Two thousand dollars."

She hung up the phone and started to cry. Then she went to her father and told him the story. They embraced and wept tears of gratefulness. When she stepped away from him, he reached into his shirt pocket, pulled out a handwritten note he composed after their earlier meeting, and gave it to her. It read: "Dear Father, you owe $2,000 for the care of your children. I love you. Jim."

I felt my pride and ego take another needed body blow as these words from Jesus came to mind, "Don't I have the right to do what I want with my own money? Or are you envious because I am generous?" (Matthew 20:15) A switch was thrown deep in my soul. I silently repented to God of my anger and unbelief. My prayer went something like this: "Dear Lord, Thank you for your provision for Sunshine Acres. I am not envious because you are generous. Actually, I am eternally grateful that you are generous! I also believe you want to make the same promise to us, so here it is. If you ever want us to have a church building—well, I'm out of ideas and, frankly, I don't have any more energy to waste on this. But I guarantee you, Father. We will never leave the nursing homes. We will continue to support Feed My Starving Children, the Dream Center, Voice of the Martyrs, and Sunshine Acres. You do whatever you want with your church. Building or not, we will continue to serve you and love them."

Within a week, I received a call from a gentleman representing an assisted living facility. He was interested in our property and was pretty confident he could get the zoning changed in his favor. He asked me for the appraisal amount.

"Eight hundred twenty thousand," I replied.

He responded, "We'll give you a lot more than that. Let me see what I can do."

He ended the call. *What? Who says that?* I thought. *Are you serious?*

He was—and so was the Lord. They went to the neighborhood association and city officials and were able to get the zoning changed. With the zoning changed our property became much more valuable. We sold the property to them for $1.4 million.

We'd been working on doing something with that chunk of desert for sixteen years. We couldn't build. We couldn't sell. And then God took care of it all—in a matter of weeks, once we completely handed it over to Him with the promise to care for widows and orphans. And now our former property is being used to care for the elderly. Our Lord is crazy good!

We met as a congregation and estimated that, with all costs figured in, the Lord had provided us with an $800,000 provision. We asked God what He wanted us to do with the money and listened for His response. Our meeting was so respectful, so gentle, that a visiting family who just happened to attend that service was so moved by our calm unity that they decided to become regular attendees. After discussion and prayer, we felt God telling us to tithe ten percent of the amount, $80,000, to Him—and that we did: $13,000 each to Feed My Starving Children, Sunshine Acres, the Dream Center, and Voice of the Martyrs. The remaining $28,000 was divided up between a dozen other ministries. What a privilege and pleasure it was to give back that much money to God and His work!

⁜

Then came a twist as we looked for a new property. A man I knew and his siblings were selling six acres of land not too far away from the previous land we owned. The property was kind of off the beaten path, but the price was right as he and I agreed on a price of $720,000. This was an astonishing price, and I was more than a little proud of myself for making it happen. I enthusiastically shared this wonderful news with our church board. We were very excited as we shared the great news with the congregation, encouraging members to go to the land, pray over it, and get ready to build! I cannot express how thrilled I was, convinced it was all in God's will and we were finally going to have a church home.

Then the man failed to return my calls. One week passed, then two. Near the end of the third week, he called my office and he sounded downright sheepish. "I was embarrassed to talk to you, Pastor," he told me. "My siblings aren't going to take $720 thousand for it."

I took a deep breath and quickly considered my options. *We had a deal. Do I call a lawyer?* "Okay—so what do they want?"

"One-point-one million."

"I don't think our church family is going to go for that," I said. He apologized again, and I knew he was being sincere. But all I wanted to do at that point was end the call. I kinda wanted to choke the guy! I disconnected—and then I yelled out loud to God. "Are you kidding me? Are we ever going to have a property that we can build on?" I vented as I'd rarely vented before and let the complaints spew, just like David did so often in Psalms. I knew God could take it. I was a little frightened and a lot mad!

"Our defiance to Jesus' command to forgive others the way we have been forgiven is why we remain in spiritual prison. Is there anyone you need to forgive from your *heart* today?"

But the Lord is so gracious and His timing is perfect. I needed to leave for one of our nursing home worship services, so I pulled myself together and was grateful that a retired pastor in our congregation was scheduled to speak to the residents at Desert Cove. As I stewed, I heard him preach about the wicked servant from Matthew 18:21-35:

"Then Peter came up and said to him, 'Lord, how often will my brother sin against me, and I forgive him? As many as seven times?' Jesus said to him, 'I do not say to you seven times, but seventy-seven times. Therefore the kingdom of heaven may be compared to a king who wished to settle accounts with his servants. When he began to settle, one was brought to him who owed him ten thousand talents. And since he could not pay, his master ordered him to be sold, with his wife and children and all that he had, and payment to be made. So the servant fell on his knees, imploring him, "Have patience with me, and I will pay you everything." And out of pity for him, the master of that servant released him and forgave him the debt. But when that same servant went out, he found one of his fellow servants who owed him a hundred denarii, and seizing him, he began to choke him, saying, "Pay what you owe." So his fellow servant fell down and pleaded with him, "Have patience with me, and I will pay you." He refused and went and put him in prison until he should pay the debt. When his fellow servants saw what had taken place, they were greatly distressed, and they went and reported to their master all that had taken place. Then his master summoned him and said to him, "You wicked servant! I forgave you all that debt because you pleaded with me. And should not you have had mercy on your fellow servant, as I had mercy on you?" And in anger his master delivered him to the jailers, until he should pay all his debt. So also my heavenly Father will do to every one of you, if you do not forgive your brother from your heart."

He concluded his message. "Consider what God has done for you. How much has He forgiven you? Our defiance to Jesus' command to forgive others the way we have been forgiven is why we remain in spiritual prison. Is there anyone you need to forgive from your *heart* today?"

I shook my head and then laughed to myself. The Lord knows precisely what we need to hear when we need to hear it. We just need to listen! Right there and then, I decided to forgive the man, and I repented to God for my anger toward the man and Him. *Alright, Lord. We're right back at it. This is your ministry, not mine. Do whatever you want. I believe you have something better for us, though I have no idea what that is. I am excited to see what your plan is. Lead the way!*

Two months later, and *one day* before we opened escrow on another piece of property for over $1 million, we received a phone call from an individual offering a six acre piece of property northeast of the intersection of Greenfield Rd. and Chandler Heights in Gilbert, AZ. He said he'd take $520,000 for it. It's worth at least twice that, located right on the corner of a major intersection! It was also a much nicer piece of property than the one we had settled on. We called a congregational meeting, prayed and discussed, and accepted the offer. Adding in payment for the cost of the street improvements adjacent to the property, the total cost was about $820,000. Or, it was supposed to be—but the seller actually agreed to pay the street improvement costs instead. That *never* happens. Board member Don Tolle said that we'd simply "continued to trust God's leading, and the seller was able to go back to the town and negotiate, come up with any amount they were willing to pay off, and still maintain the offer price we had agreed on. It took patience and knowing that God's in charge. There was a lot of faith and prayer going into it."

So, in no more than a ten month period, the Lord provided a buyer for our old property at twice the price we hoped to receive, a new piece of property at half what we thought we would pay, and included the street improvements paid by the seller! The total financial provision was well over two million dollars, and we were able to begin building a facility for our church home. What did we do to *make* this happen? Absolutely nothing. We just gave it up. We promised the Lord we would focus like a laser on listening to Jesus, caring for orphans and widows, and let Him know we were fine with whatever He wanted to do with His ministry. Everything was done by Him, in His time, and in His way. The Holy Spirit made it all happen, so He gets all the glory!

The Lord was not done providing for His new building just yet. Steve Vincent, one of the men in our men's ministry, works for a commercial property development company. Through his company all of our carpet, ninety percent of the lighting, and all of our cabinets and counters as well as all of the sinks were donated! The Lord provided so much through Steve and his company that we had quite a bit left over. We joyfully passed the blessing on to Sunshine Acres, and they used much of the blessing in the new cafeteria they were building. Thank you, Lord! Brent Grimes, also a leader in our men's ministry, was able to get all of our chairs for the sanctuary donated. Our men, women, and children served and served, putting in tons of "sweat equity." When the building was completed, the architect said it came in almost $300,000 less than anticipated. Our first worship service in our new building was this past Christmas Eve. We received our certificate of occupancy at two o'clock that afternoon. The first service was at 6:00 p.m. God is always right on time!

We never know how much pressure we are under until we are out from under it, set free to love God and serve others, and to finally become the new creation in Christ we were always meant to be. I carried the financial and building burdens of the ministry for so long because I truly believed I was supposed to! I never knew they were His to carry until the Lord brought me to Sunshine Acres, showing us an astonishing alternative. There was no way to deny the Lord's provision for them. Could it be that simple? Yes—and praise be to God! I would never have believed the Lord would do something like that for us, until He did. The freedom is ridiculous.

When we repent and come back to life in Christ, rededicate our lives and ministries to the Lord, being perfectly content with however large or small He wants to grow them, and then restructure our lives and ministries around listening to Jesus, He refocuses our attention to truly care for hurting people. The Holy Spirit begins pouring out miracles of life transformation and provision. What is left but to praise and thank Him? As the closing verse in the psalms shouts out across the millennia, "Let everything that has breath praise the Lord! Praise the Lord!" (Psalm 150:6) As long as I have breath in my body, may it be a breath of praise!

Chapter 12

For I know the plans I have for you, declares the Lord,
plans for welfare and not for evil, to give you a future
and a hope. Then you will call upon me and come and pray
to me, and I will hear you. You will seek me and find me,
when you seek me with all your heart.
JEREMIAH 29:11-13

Money is nothing to God. Let me repeat that. Money is *nothing* to God. He owns it all and is not worried about it in any way. However, hurting people mean *everything* to Him. My problem was that I had those completely reversed. I thought getting enough money and building was the key to ministry, and then we would, when the time was right, get around to caring for the hurting people. Or would we?

The Holy Spirit reminds us of the words of Jesus, just as our Savior promised: "Therefore do not be anxious, saying, 'What shall we eat?' or 'What shall we drink?' or 'What shall we wear?' For the Gentiles seek after all these things, and your heavenly Father knows that you need them all. But seek first the kingdom of God and his righteousness, and all these things will be added to you." (Matthew 6:31-33) This is still our Father's world. He knows we have a tendency to worry about ourselves, and yet the Spirit gives us the faith to get out of own way so we can care for the least, the lost, and the hurting. That is a huge part of His "righteousness." As we listen, trust and obey Him, the Holy Spirit transforms us to be more like Jesus and provides *everything* needed for ministry. Is financial provision included in "all these things?" Absolutely!

The faithful servants at Camp Aloma in Prescott, AZ know this to be true.

Light of Christ had been going up to Camp Aloma, a gorgeous mountain site with a mission to provide people, places and programs pointing to Christ, on a regular basis for years when then camp president Bob McNaughton asked me in 2013 to consider joining their board of directors and invited me to attend a meeting. I agreed. The meeting was dominated by a discussion on financial issues, the need for added fundraisers, and other worries—and as the session neared the end of its second hour, I sat tight and doodled on both sides of the agenda page. I thought, *Lord Jesus, help me! Either the meeting needs to end or you need to get me more paper.* As the meeting neared its close, Bob looked at me.

"Would you like to add anything, Pastor Moe?"

I remained silent for a moment. "Yeah, I think I would. I think we need to give this ministry back to Jesus. It belongs to Him. That means the burden is His. If we do what He is calling us to do, He'll take care of all of this other stuff."

I was not being flippant; I was dead serious. And I knew that how everyone responded in the next few seconds was going to reveal whether or not they wanted to explore what a Spirit-led ministry looks like. The potential for any ministry is beyond belief when it is given back to the Lord. Then, one by one, each person nodded their heads. Next thing I knew, I was leading Bob and the board in a prayer of repentance and rededication as they gave Camp Aloma back to God. I joined their board shortly after that.

Things started happening pretty quickly. It was just a few months later, about a week before Light of Christ was due to go to the camp, that I was trying to get in touch with the camp director and he wasn't returning my calls or emails. I knew he was a young man with a family, and I imagined how difficult it must be to live at camp and run it. Yet I was frustrated, so I started praying, asking the Lord to soften my heart and to help the director if anything was wrong. It was then that I felt the Holy Spirit tell me, "If he ever steps down, Leah would be ideal."

Leah was Leah McKean. She'd been coming to Camp Aloma since she was seven. She had served the camp as junior staff, youth counselor, kitchen staff, and a senior counselor for three summers. She had also worked at United Cerebral Palsy where she was certified to help special needs children. Countless times, I had seen her talking with or holding a child if he or she were having trouble adjusting to the camp. I knew she had incredible gifts, a great love for Jesus, and a heart for the camp. She was young, though, younger even than the man currently serving as the director. Because of his age, I figured he'd easily be there for another decade or so. "Alright, Lord," I said in prayer. "When he steps down, which probably won't happen for another ten years, I hope Leah is still around." Just two days later, I got a call from Bob. He was clearly concerned.

I told him about my prayer time with
our Father two days earlier and
what I believed was a clear word from Him.

"Pastor Moe, are you sitting down?"

"No," I said, "but hit me. What's going on?"

"The camp director just resigned."

"What!" I replied.

"I know," Bob said, exasperated. "If we don't have enough problems already, now we're going to have to do a national search and—"

I let him vent for a couple of minutes. Then I said, "Look. I'm not saying we won't need to do that, but I think the person God has for this leadership position is already at camp."

"Who?" he asked.

"Leah."

He was silent for a moment, as though he were stunned. "She's so young," he countered.

"And that doesn't matter. She has incredible leadership gifts and love for this ministry.   As long as she's not micromanaging, and she's young enough to not have learned that yet, the Lord will show all of us where we fit in this ministry. And we will all encourage each other. I believe it will be incredible!" I told him about my prayer time with our Father two days earlier and what I believed was a clear word from Him.

"Oh my goodness," he said. "Could it be?"

"I've never seen anyone as naturally gifted as this young lady. I absolutely believe this is of God."

We agreed to pray about it and then met with Leah the following week. We asked her to prayerfully consider taking the camp directorship, and she says that's exactly what she did. Every chance she got, Leah went off by herself to get away from the distractions of her camp duties and talk with God. "I opened up my Bible and read whatever came to me. Sometimes I would cry and ask the Lord, 'Is this what you want?' I wanted to listen to Him." We reassured her that we'd get other people to serve in any areas where she didn't feel gifted or qualified.

Leah started on an interim basis and took the position as her own within a month. Today she maintains the role and lives at the camp. "With every financial need, God has provided just what was needed. There is humility and patience in that. He has me here for a reason whether it's for five years or for the rest of my life." God met a staffing need, putting the right person from within the organization in the best place of leadership, a hallmark of Spirit-led ministry.

Not long after that, we learned that the church that owned Camp Aloma was being bought out. The new buyers could do whatever they wanted with the camp. However, the owner agreed to sign over the deed to the other member congregations of the camp prior to the buyout. The camp's estimated worth is $1.5 million. I figured the church would charge at least a couple hundred thousand dollars for the deed. But it asked for no money; it's only condition was that the member congregations provide ten scholarships a year to inner city kids, the very thing we had a desire to do. Praise God!

Then, eight months later, another church that was being sold named us the recipient of a portion of the sale. It had no other affiliation with Camp Aloma except for triplets who participated in camp during the summer. We had no idea how much the church had decided to give the camp. However, we realized how hard it is on the members and leadership of a congregation when it has to close. We sent word out to encourage as many people as possible from the camp ministry to show up at the service where proceeds were to be handed out. We felt compelled to love these folks, thank them for their decision to support Camp Aloma, and let them know their donation would make a huge difference.

The afternoon of the service we comprised one-third of those in attendance, which included members from the congregation that was closing as well as representatives from the nine other ministries receiving checks. When our name was called, Bob went up, said a word or two about the camp, thanked the church, and then returned to his seat next to me. He showed me the envelope. The amount of the check inside was written on the front: $95,400. Glory to God!

I later learned that this miracle was aided by the youngest of those triplets. Her name is Kirsten and she'd been coming to the camp every summer since she was seven. She was the one who told her church leadership about the camp, what it meant to her and her siblings, and requested that a portion of the sale be given to Camp Aloma. Now eighteen, Kirsten is a senior counselor at the camp, something she says she's always wanted to do to nurture the kid's "relentless" faith and have it rub off on her.

"The joy that they had when they praised God was just inspiring as a young kid. My favorite part of camp was singing and praising God around the campfire. God became more palpable as I was surrounded by like-minded people trying to help me on my faith journey." The year her church closed, Kirsten learned to play guitar at the camp and sometimes led worship. "The sound of the kid's voices coming back with such overwhelming power and grace was wonderful. Even though that was such a terrible time to go through, coming to camp allowed me to hear from God, 'I'm not going away,' He told me. 'I'm going to be with you.'"

Our Heavenly Father spoke to His precious daughter, a teenager named Kirsten, and then through her to His other children in the congregation. He led them to give almost one hundred thousand dollars in support of a ministry that had gone through this process: repented and rededicated itself to Jesus, restructured the ministry around the Word of God, refocused on helping hurting people, and now rejoiced in His provision of leadership and finances. The Lord works in mysterious and awesome ways!

Camp Aloma now offers free weekends for those who cannot afford the camp experience. Leah, Bob, and their staff and volunteers are thriving, as is the camp. The camp is now offering free weekends for women and their children from a Phoenix women's shelter. Leah has mentioned how she would love begin tithing to other ministries so Camp Aloma can be a blessing to them. All of this from a ministry that literally two years earlier some had considered closing for half of the year because of finances!

⁂

Eric Meissner is a dear friend of mine and an incredible encourager. We've known each other for almost thirty years and went to seminary together. He is now pastor of Trinity Lutheran Church in Avoca, Iowa. He says he has seen the Lord transform him as he has allowed God to work in his life to create, as he put it, "less of me and more of Him."

"As pastors, we are called to be spiritual leaders," he says. "Those who were burned out and have regained their strength have done so because they've become spiritual leaders. It frees you to know that you don't have to know all of the answers, but God does. He's just waiting for us to let go. The more you can point people to what God is doing in their life and in their church, the more they trust you as their pastor and spiritual leader. It's a matter of gaining people's trust, and you do that as you trust in the Lord."

Eric says he and his church have learned a wonderful truth. "The Kingdom of God is upside down and backwards. When you trust Him, He provides," he says. "We started a clothing and food pantry, and there were times we didn't have any money. I kept saying, 'If we give this away, God will give to us in return.' They've seen how God has replenished the storehouse. His ways are not the world's ways. The more we give, the more we get. That's when you see that spiritual shift of people getting on God's agenda, where they say, 'I want more of releasing God in my life to experience His presence and provision.'"

Most of all, Eric has watched as God has transformed the people of Trinity Lutheran. "I've seen the church move from selfishness to servanthood. Once, we were really into fundraising; we'd have several events each year. That's fallen by the wayside to move to outreach events. Every month through the summer we have Super Summer Saturdays, where we invite the community to our parking lot, have a carnival for the kids, and give away clothes and food," he says. "We also have Back to School Night where we give away backpacks to kids along with the supplies they need. It's been such a paradigm shift from taking care of ourselves to taking care of those God has called us to serve; following His agenda."

> The Holy Spirit helped the entire ministry at
> Trinity transition from fear to faith, anxiety to joy,
> money to ministry, and from saving to giving.

Eric and I were talking on the phone a few months back, encouraging each other in our walks with Jesus, when Eric said in an off-hand way, "Our church council decided last night that we are sitting on too much money. We decided to give most of our savings away." This got my attention. You don't normally hear pastors say such things.

He continued, "We decided to work toward giving a certain amount to each of our ministry teams, and then they can decide where to give it. So our youth ministry will receive some, children's ministry, women's ministry, etcetera, and they are all going to pray and then direct that money to the hurting people God puts on their hearts." I told him that sounded like an incredible idea. What a fantastic way to develop that spirit of joyful giving at every level in the congregation!

But there was something I had to know. "How much did you decide to give away?" He answered, "Our goal is ninety-five thousand dollars."

What? Talk about putting your money where your mouth is. "We decided to let Jesus be our rainy-day fund and to give His financial blessings away." The Holy Spirit has transformed their ministry, beginning with the leaders, from focusing on several fundraisers a year to a goal of giving away $95,000! The vote on the council was unanimous. Glory to God!

The Holy Spirit helped the entire ministry at Trinity transition from fear to faith, anxiety to joy, money to ministry, and from saving to giving. God continues to meet their financial needs, just as He had for Light of Christ's property situation, just as He had for Sunshine Acres for over sixty years, just as He had for Camp Aloma—and just as He does for *any* ministry that chooses to be Spirit-led and allows the Holy Spirit to do the difficult, refining work of *becoming* Spirit-led. A very simple principle is this: The Spirit provides what the Spirit guides. Could it be this simple? Absolutely and praise be to God!

We do believe, Lord Jesus. Help us overcome our unbelief! (Mark 9:24)

Chapter 13

And Jesus answered them, "Those who are well have
no need of a physician, but those who are sick."
LUKE 5:31

He'd built his business from the ground up for two decades, but now it was gone—and Jeff Clark was spiritually, physically, emotionally, and mentally exhausted. He'd come to the end of himself. Despair from the loss of his business, worry for the future and how to support his family, and an inability to focus in the midst of all of the anxiety was overwhelming him.

A friend invited Jeff to attend one of our men's Bible discussion groups. As Jeff began to look to Jesus, the Lord began to bring him out of the darkness. He wrote the following email to me, his family, and the friend who invited him to the Bible group just a few weeks after he started attending the discussions. It is simply the most beautiful email I have ever received. It should be noted that at the time Jeff said he was so anxious he couldn't even write up a resume. Rejoice as you read his words.

Our Heavenly Father is working in my life and heaping gifts of peace and joy on me so fast that I can hardly keep up. My prayer time this morning was filled entirely with expressions of thankfulness...for the fire doing its work in me over the past weeks and for the blessings He has provided so generously and so soon in this journey. That this could be my spirit less than eight weeks from my darkest days marks a miracle so striking to me. As I prayed this morning, I did not have an impulse to ask for anything. How could I have so far to go yet be so satisfied in this moment? God has shown up for me in such a big way and the answer to those prayers today was that I ought to share [this email with you].

On September 10, a paragraph from my devotion read, "There is a divine mystery in suffering, one that has a strange and supernatural power and has never been completely understood by human reason. No one has ever developed a deep level of spirituality or holiness without experiencing a great deal of suffering. When a person who suffers reaches a point where he can be calm and carefree, inwardly smiling at his own suffering, and no longer asking God to be delivered from it, then the suffering has accomplished its blessed ministry, perseverance has finished its work, and the crucifixion has begun to weave itself into a crown." September 10 would have been a few days before executing the final agreement that gave me closure for the future of my company and the beginning of the end of my relationship with it, and ushered in a new personal, professional, and family struggle of life change and unknown. This was a crowded time, filled with the busy work of completing and negotiating a sound agreement in a very short time. My mind, body, and spirit were depleted to the point of brokenness. By this time, I had begun to take steps in faith, knowing from memory of the Spirit's past work in me that hearing Him again was my only way forward. While I could understand this logically, my mind and heart were noisy places where His voice had been drowned out. His work had begun, but it was too soon for me to believe I could have the spirit described in this devotion, expect it, and look forward to it. It was not too soon, though, for me to be challenged to pray for it [and] to work to believe it.

Day by day, bit by bit, through the good and bad days since, He has rewarded my steps with faith to take new steps. New steps have been rewarded with measures of grace and peace. Gradual healing of body and mind have given me a stronger, longer stride to these steps which, in turn, have been rewarded with more grace [and] more peace. Particularly, in the last couple of weeks, more so in the last week, and especially today, I am realizing that the measures of grace and peace have outnumbered the measures of fear and worry. In fact, on this day the fear and worry are nowhere to be found; they'll be back and there is much healing and uncertainty to *be dealt with, but I know now that these spiritual gifts have grown despite the bad days...and there have been some of our most difficult moments in the past week. Praise God! His ways are resilient to our greatest trials. It appears our knowledge of His strength is proportional to the greatest trial we have yet faced...[it] would be easier if it weren't this way, but I am thankful for the rewards, however they come.*

Your prayers and encouragement have instructed me and anticipated this specifically. I am so thankful for those prayers and encouragement and for God's work in your lives that you could believe this when I couldn't. [My wife] Chris and I look forward to your continued prayers and encouragement. Our family also faces its greatest trial and hungers for the same gifts. Our Lord will provide. –Jeff

Jeff's testimony is a reminder to all of us of what God can do when we finally come to the end of ourselves, give our lives back to Jesus, learn how to listen to Him and then follow Him. This is why the top of my daily to-do list is "funeral and resurrection"—to die to self and be raised in Holy Spirit power. As Jeff was heading to the office for the last time, boxes at the ready to clean out his desk, he received a phone call. He pulled to the side of the road to talk. An hour and a half later he had a new job. He never even got around to creating a resume. God is so very good!

We all agreed that a big part of becoming spiritually healthy is to stop blaming others because we have taken our eyes off of Jesus!

Make no mistake. Actually doing these things consistently and living the life the Lord intends for us is *hard*. If it was easy everyone would be living it! In Matthew 7:13-14, Jesus tells us to "enter by the narrow gate. For the gate is wide and the way is easy that leads to destruction, and those who enter by it are many. For the gate is narrow and the way is hard that leads to life, and those who find it are few."

But Lord, what about the *easy* yoke and *light* burden?

Once we are yoked with Jesus, following His lead and in His power, it is easy and light. Even putting on His yoke when everything has fallen apart is kind of easy because our options are severely limited. However, submitting to put on His yoke every day and every minute of every day once things are back to normal is *very* hard. It is also the path to life. Praise the Lord to be surrounded by people who understand this dynamic and can help each other! Dying to self to be raised in Christ is completely opposite what the world says. It is opposite what our sin nature says. But remember; you are not alone. The Holy Spirit is with you and will use others to help you. No condemnation; just encouragement. The more we can help one another to return to Jesus, rededicate our lives and ministries to Him, daily put on His yoke, and humbly walk with Him as we serve others, the more our souls are healed and find rest in Him. Praise God for our faith family!

About fifteen years ago, Pastor Paul Witkop and I felt led by the Lord to put together a twenty-four hour retreat for pastors and their spouses, and it had absolutely nothing to do with "church growth." Paul had discovered a wonderful teaching on DVD from Andy Stanley of North Point Community Church. His focus on sustainable pace was a big part of the presentation. We felt led by the Spirit to use the teaching as a springboard to focus on two main questions:

1. How's your walk with your Heavenly Father?
2. How's your walk with your spouse?

If those two are strong, it doesn't matter what we come up against, because the Lord will bring us through. We asked that everyone refrain from complaining, bragging, or even talking about their ministries. How is your walk with our Father? How is your walk with your spouse? That is it. We also looked at different biblical passages to guide us.

People were beside themselves as they filled out the evaluations at the end. The positives were at least ten-to-one over the negatives. The Spirit showed up in a powerful, beautiful way. One of the more revealing questions during our wrap-up time was this: "How can we have this same peace, joy and love when we go back to our ministries, realizing that the entire ministry culture around us is sick?" We all agreed that a big part of becoming spiritually healthy is to stop blaming others because we have taken our eyes off of Jesus! Turn around and return to His arms of love, not with guilt or shame, but joy in the knowledge that He's already died to set us free. He has never given up on us. Focus on Jesus. No more excuses. Return to your first love. Give the ministry back to Him. He gets both the glory and the burdens. Then follow Jesus and lead by example. It may take a while, but remember: it is the Holy Spirit's job to transform His ministry, not ours. The Spirit will grow in us patience and gentleness as He is working it all out. And we will be front and center to witness His miracles of astonishing transformation.

The Spirit also encourages us through the faith of other family members we won't meet until the Lord brings us home to heaven. Pastor Richard Wurmbrand is the founder of "Voices of the Martyrs." He was in a communist prison for over fourteen years because of his love for Jesus and commitment to sharing the gospel with everyone. The following is an excerpt from a book he wrote in three days after his release from prison. It's entitled "Tortured for Christ" and I cannot recommend it highly enough. Notice how they helped and encouraged one another.

It was strictly forbidden to preach to other prisoners, as it is in captive nations today. It was understood that whoever was caught doing this received a severe beating. A number of us decided to pay the price for the privilege of preaching, so we accepted their terms. It was a deal: we preached and they beat us. We were happy preaching; they were happy beating us—so everyone was happy.

The following scene happened more times than I can remember. A brother was preaching to the other prisoners when the guards suddenly burst in, surprising him halfway through a phrase. They hauled him down the corridor to their "beating room." After what seemed an endless beating, they brought him back and threw him—bloody and bruised—on the prison floor. Slowly, he picked up his battered body, painfully straightened his clothing, and said, "Now, brethren, where did I leave off when I was interrupted?" He continued his gospel message!

Our problem in the free world is different from the challenges for our persecuted brothers and sisters. Our problem is distraction, isolation and listening to voices other than the Good Shepherd's voice. Pray for our persecuted family, as well as their persecutors, and take heart! As we care for them, they are also caring for us. How?

A few years ago some Christians from America had a meeting with some Christians from North Korea, where it is estimated that over 30,000 followers of Jesus are in concentration camps this very day. The meeting was held in China. The North Korean followers of the Good Shepherd had snuck across the border for this time of prayer, encouragement, and fellowship. As they were about to return to their countries one of the men from America told them, "Please let our brothers and sisters in North Korea know that we are praying for them." The representatives from the family of God from North Korea expressed their thanks for this.

Then one of them replied, "And please let our brothers and sisters in America know that we are praying for you, too." One of the Americans responded, "Thank you. But what do you pray for us?" He answered, "Well, in North Korea all we have is Jesus. We have learned all we need is Jesus. But in America, since you have so much, we are afraid you may not know that all you need is Jesus. So we are praying for you to *know* that all you need is Jesus."

How humbling and encouraging to know these precious people are praying for us to focus solely on Jesus, and help others to do the same. Some are praying for us right now from their prison cells!

✥

At the Special Olympics track and field event held in Spokane, Washington in 1976, nine contestants, all physically or mentally disabled, assembled at the starting line for the 100-yard dash. At the gun, they all started out, not exactly in a dash, but clearly with a desire to run the race to the finish and win. They were doing well.

All, that is, except one little boy who stumbled on the asphalt, tumbled over a couple of times, and began to cry. Two of the other contestants heard his cries, slowed down, stopped, turned, and went back to him. They helped him up and the three of them walked arm-in-arm to the finish line. Everyone in the stadium stood and cheered. The cheering went on and on and on.

This is a remarkable story for a variety of reasons, not the least of which is that the first time it was told to me, there was a slight variation. In that version, *all* of the runners stopped and walked arm-in-arm to the finish line. However, after a little research it became clear that although this is the more popular version of what transpired, the truth is only two other runners helped their fallen competitor. Why didn't the others stop? Perhaps they didn't hear his cries. Maybe they were so focused on running the race and trying to win, their first priority was to finish the race despite his cries. They could always check on him after they crossed the line. That would likely have been my reaction.

We don't know why the others didn't respond. All we do know is that two did stop, go back, help him up, and walk together to the finish line. And this is what people remember. Why? Because I believe this touches the God-created part of us; the eternal part of us. The part that wants to follow Jesus to broken, hurting, helpless people, even if it means laying aside goals we've had for a long time. Even if it means not winning the race. Even if it means coming in last.

The Bible speaks of a race in Hebrews 12:1-2. "Therefore, since we are surrounded by so great a cloud of witnesses, let us also lay aside every weight, and sin which clings so closely, and let us run with endurance the race that is set before us, looking to Jesus, the founder and perfecter of our faith, who for the joy that was set before him endured the cross, despising the shame, and is seated at the right hand of the throne of God."

The race we are running is never against other people. It is a race of endurance that has been marked out for us. It is a race that can only be run as we keep our eyes on Jesus. It is a race that involves carrying a cross like our Savior, following Him, and helping others. It is powered by the Holy Spirit. Those who have gone before us are cheering us on from heaven! How incredible if we could learn how to cheer each other on as well *while we are still here.* Is it possible to join that heavenly chorus here on Earth? Some already have. Will we join in?

Can you imagine how beautiful it can be if Jesus gives us the ears to hear the cries of other spiritual leaders, brothers and sisters who have stumbled and fallen? What about the cries of our brothers and sisters in persecuted countries? Think how amazing it can be if we allowed ourselves no excuses to leave them behind? How blessed by God the entire church worldwide can be if we stopped, went back, helped them up, and walked together across the finish line—not to mention allowing them to help us up when we fall? Imagine if ministry leaders can stop competing and comparing ourselves with each other (this is demonic) and instead start to truly reach out to each other in love, encouraging and praying for each other! I believe Jesus wants us to help each other. Can there be any doubt? Will you be the one through whom Jesus reaches out to His other ministry leaders in your area, loving and encouraging them?

We are not called to be great pastors,
whatever that means. We are called to become
great servants as we are discipled by the greatest
Servant of all through the pure power of the Holy Spirit.

As we listen to Jesus He will show us how to pray, encourage, support, love, and laugh with one another—all the while giving God all of the glory He deserves as we joyfully serve the least and the lost in our communities. In return, our Father will give us all of the power, peace and joy we will ever need while He builds His ministries His way, complimenting each other but never competing.

During my first year in the parish, I had lunch one day with a fellow pastor. He had served in many settings and was closing in on retirement. We both served small, inner city congregations at the time. We talked about a variety of things. There was a lull in the conversation when he looked out the window and, with a clearly heavy heart, said with resignation, "I have come to the conclusion that I will never be a great pastor."

I imagine I said a few words to try and encourage him. I didn't really know how to respond at that point in my life and ministry. However, I do remember what I was thinking. *You're probably right. Your retirement is right around the corner. But me? I am going to be a great pastor!*

The reason I remember those thoughts so clearly from twenty years ago is that now I know what to say. We are not called to be great pastors, whatever that means. We are called to become great *servants* as we are discipled by the greatest Servant of all through the pure power of the Holy Spirit. If that means serving a small, inner city ministry with the heart of Jesus, praise God for that small, inner-city ministry and that our Father chose you to serve there! What a challenge and an incredible honor! The Lord obviously believes in you and what the two of you will do together. Shine the light of Christ in that darkness. Give your life and ministry back to Jesus every day. Love everybody with the extraordinary, extravagant Holy Spirit love within you! Give God the glory!

The Holy Spirit changes the way we look at everything. If you were to ask the members of Light of Christ to describe what "growth" means to them, many will tell you it is "the transformation of the human heart, one heart at a time," as Jesus saves, heals, restores, and lets us know that we possess incredible *value* in Him. Everyone matters to Him. Absolutely everyone! We pray for the Lord to send us broken, hurting people and we promise to love them. So He does.

Scott and Jenn Paul started coming to Light of Christ in February 2016 in the wake of personal tragedy. She had just had a miscarriage—and their pain from the loss of baby Caroline was still raw. Originally from a Catholic background, they had tried attending several parishes and other churches, but never felt like they fit in. Through a Google search, Jenn discovered our website and saw we did a lot of outreach to the community. She liked that, along with the fact that we were nearby. Still on bed rest and prompted by Scott's expressed need to find a church to attend, they visited us one morning. "We came and everybody was friendly," she said. "They were also doing good things for others less fortunate. I thought that was amazing. It's doing what God wants people to do."

Jenn said the Lord used the Spirit-led mission and people of the church to bring healing and hope to her broken heart. "It was just a sense of comfort," she said. "It was just a couple of weeks after coming the pastor wanted to have a service for Caroline. I thought, 'Why would he want to do that for someone who's not a member of the church?'"

Scott said he was overwhelmed by the love he and his wife experienced. "When we lost Caroline, I found myself reaching out to God, just evaluating and starting to think, 'What is this life all about?' The acceptance and love that exists here—we were like family immediately and I'd never felt that in a church before." He also embraced Light of Christ's emphasis to serve others. "Since February, I've done more for others than in my entire life."

One of the ways Scott and his family served others was through Feed My Starving Children, and the Holy Spirit immediately spoke to their beautiful daughter, Grace. "We went and she said to us, 'I've got an idea. I want to feed a family of four for a year.'" Scott said. "She started texting her friends right away."

"Just knowing I can help," Grace added, "and that simple things add up—it's like a win-win. You feel benefitted, but you know someone else is benefitted." Grace just did a fundraiser completely on her own, raising almost a thousand dollars for FMSC. God is so good.

The next Sunday after Jenn and Scott started attending Light of Christ, they invited her mother Lori. "I was born and raised Catholic, from Chicago, and the kids went to Catholic schools and that's what I've always learned," Lori said. "We were always told what the nuns taught us and what the priest taught us, but we never really opened a Bible." Not only did she feel welcomed like Jenn and Scott did, but Lori started attending a Bible discussion group. They all did. "I feel closer to God," Lori said, holding back tears. "I've learned to forgive. I'm a better person. It's hard, but I've learned. This church is so comforting to me, and I know it is to Jenn and Scott and Grace, and I just want us to get closer because we need to be. Because one day we're all gonna be together with Caroline."

Do you realize there is a group of hurting, broken people who are praying that someone, somewhere will bring them *true* hope and love? They are hidden from the world and often they will hide from the world. But they are there. Jesus has not forgotten them. He knows where they are. Just like with Jen, Scott, Grace, and Lori, God will use you to love others like them, to encourage them, never give up on them, and be their friend.

Listen to Jesus. He will love you to life and show you where you fit. He will break your heart for the people you are to love. He is calling out to you through them! He is waving His arms to get your attention. He will fill you with so much of His perfect love that you will forget you were ever afraid. And He will lead you to them. Simply pour, pour, pour His love into them. And oh, how beautiful you will be, to those broken, hurting, lonely, lost, and precious people when they meet you and see Jesus in you.

A follower of the Good Shepherd went to a Pakistani jail to visit a brother in Christ recently arrested for telling others about Jesus. He stepped up to the counter. The officer looked him in the eyes and said, "You are here to visit your friend, aren't you?"

"Yes, I am," responded the disciple of Jesus.

"Follow me." Without another word the officer led him past numerous cells, stopped at one, took out his keys and opened the door, walked past other prisoners and led him directly to his friend in the cell.

"How did you know that he is the one I came to see?" inquired the gentlemen.

"You are Christians, correct?" the officer responded. They nodded their heads. "I thought so. Your faces are different."

The people you are called to care for are waiting to see Jesus in your blessed, beautiful and loving face. They may be at the hospital or the homeless shelter. They could be waiting for you and Jesus at the orphanage, the nursing home, or the jail cell. They might misread the sign you're holding, thinking you're giving away hogs. They might get your heart in a mission overseas or downtown. They might be waiting for someone who truly knows and loves Jesus to knock on their door, not for our sake but for their sake. They might be standing behind a business counter when you give them the greatest gift they have ever received, encouraging them to open the Bible and read about the Lover of their souls. They might be your coworker or neighbor, prepared by the Holy Spirit for your invitation to read and discuss the words and life of this one man, Jesus, in a safe and pressure free setting. They might be living in a cave! They might be completely unaware of being lost at all, but Jesus will lead you to them with a holy fire and love that, if nothing else confuses them and peeks their interest.

Pastor Moe, God is so good to me!
He loves me so much, but you know what, brother?
He loves you so much, too!

Are you ready? Listen to Jesus. Truly listen to Jesus. He loves you! He has an adventure that only the two of you can live together. Only He knows what it is. It is your calling. It is good, pleasing and perfect. It is so beautiful, powerful and sacrificial that you'll willingly give your life for it! Listen to Jesus and don't worry about being like anyone else. Allow Him to make you uniquely you. It is the life the first disciples knew. It is the life our persecuted brothers and sisters are living right now. Listen to Jesus and then follow Him in the pure power of the Holy Spirit.

"How then will they call on him in whom they have not believed? And how are they to believe in him of whom they have never heard? And how are they to hear without someone preaching? And how are they to preach unless they are sent? As it is written, "How beautiful are the feet of those who preach the good news!" (Romans 10:14-15)

One of my favorite sayings is something I learned a long time ago: "Preach the gospel at all times. When necessary use words." Actions speak much louder than words. Lord Jesus, show us how to preach the good news of your love and salvation at *all* times.

✢

The worship service at the care facility concluded. A couple of our regular attendees were not there, so I went to check on them. John was not in his room, so I assumed he was doing physical therapy. I was disappointed, not just because I loved John but because every time I went to encourage him, he ended up encouraging me! The staff told me this was not unusual: John encouraged everyone! A normal conversation with him went something like this:

"John, how are you doing today, brother?"

"Pastor Moe, God is so good to me! He loves me so much, but you know what, brother? He loves you so much, too! You are a blessing to me. You are a beautiful, powerful man of God and, ooooh boy, is Jesus using you! I see Him in you! I cannot tell you how much I love you, Pastor Moe!"

I always chuckled, shook my head, and smiled ear to ear. "John, you always bless me with your love for Jesus and your love for me. You absolutely shine the light of Christ. Thank you, brother."

I was thinking of this astonishing brother in Christ as I headed for the exit. I passed by the dining room, glanced in, and there was John—sitting at a table getting ready for lunch. I immediately turned in to say, "Hi!" to my dear friend. He shared the joy of the Lord with me as always, but then he asked, "Pastor Moe, I know you are a busy man, but do you have time for a story?"

"John, I will stay as long as you like," I told him as I made myself comfortable in the seat next to him. "Tell me your story."

He shared about his son, Timothy. John said that his son was in prison and would not be getting out for thirty-three years. "Oh, John, I am so sorry. How long has Timothy had problems with the law?"

"On and off since he was nineteen," John responded. "He is fifty now."

That took my breath away. Began at nineteen and won't get out until he's eighty-three. Goodness.

"What was it?" I asked, wondering what drew Timothy to lawlessness.

"Drugs," John answered, and then continued. "I've learned something, Pastor Moe. Drugs don't just destroy the person. They destroy the whole family. His mother and I have been on our knees praying for him for decades. We love him so much. We just pray and pray and pray and pray. Only Jesus can save Him. There was nothing else we could do."

It was at that moment I made the connection. Anyone with the kind of faith, hope, love, and joy that John has must have gone through incredibly rough times. You don't get faith of that depth with an easy life, just like body builders don't get all those muscles sitting on the couch! You don't get that level of faith in Jesus until you know Jesus is all you have and all you need. You don't get that astonishing love from man. It pours from the throne of our Heavenly Father. You don't have the kind of hope that John has until you know the beautiful Savior very, very well, and that nothing is too big for Him. And although John was in a very difficult life situation, the Holy Spirit filled him with a joy I have rarely witnessed.

There are some Christians who use phrases like "Praise the Lord" and "God is good" simply as an expression of speech—but there are others for whom those words seem to come from the essence of their being, from their very soul! John was such a person. He didn't simply say, "Praise be to God!" He exuded it! His love for the Lord was an essential part of his entire being. Now it began to make sense. Here is a broken-hearted man whose Lord had healed his broken heart again and again and again. John got knocked down and the Spirit picked him back up! He had learned to submit under the mighty hand of God, and joy was his reward.

Yet I began to get anxious about what was coming next, because I knew there was more to the story. Tears filled his eyes as he continued.

"This week I got a letter from Timothy. An eight page letter!" John then went on to describe that it wasn't just any letter. It was *the* letter—the one that told his dad that he had given his life to Jesus! In it, Timothy poured out his heart, his love, and his appreciation to his earthly father. It was filled with praises for God, love for Jesus, love for his family, and apologies for all of the hurt he had caused. He had asked Jesus into his heart, and even though he was still in a physical prison, he had finally been set free—from his past, from his sins, and from his excuses. Set free to love! Timothy thanked his earthly father for never giving up and always praying for him!

My heart overflowed with praise and I wept tears for my dear friend, John. He was beside himself! His love for his son was overwhelming! He thanked Jesus again and again as tears of joy cascaded down his cheeks. It remains one of the great honors in my life to have shared those moments with John.

My guess is some might question the validity of Timothy's jailhouse conversion. I understand that. No doubt, some jailhouse conversions are an act with a hidden (and sometimes not so hidden) agenda. Yet how is that any different from conversions outside of prison walls? I have a friend who confesses that he has been baptized three different times, "each for a different girl." However, I believe there is a higher percentage of heartfelt, soul-altering, eternal life transforming, Holy Spirit powered, *genuine* conversions in prison cells than there are in church pews! When a person spends twenty-three hours a day in a four-by-eight foot cell, it gives plenty of time to look back over one's life and decisions, and plenty of time to consider some of the deeper questions in life. It affords a person the opportunity to do the only necessary thing we have been discussing in this book: quieting down and listening to Jesus. When you mix in plenty of time on your hands with an opportunity to read about Jesus and His life as well as a good dose of humility, the Holy Spirit can work the miraculous!

John shared that he hoped he'd be able to see his son again before he died, but admitted that was looking rather unlikely. Then he shared these words from Timothy's letter: "We may not see each other again on this side, dad. But we will all be together in Heaven forever. Thank you with all my heart! Thank you for never quitting on me. Thank you for praying for me! I love you so much! I am free! I owe everything to Jesus!"

At that point I could hardly speak. I gave John a huge hug. Once I was able to compose myself, I asked, "John, would it be okay if I shared your story with our church family on Sunday?"

His eyes bored into mine and he spoke with an unmistakable, supernatural power and conviction, "Pastor Moe—tell *everyone*."

So I am. Or at least I'm trying.

Chapter 14

*Rejoice always, pray without ceasing, give thanks
in all circumstances; for this is the will of God in
Christ Jesus for you. Do not quench the Spirit.*
1 Thessalonians 5:16-19

'll never forget when, six years ago on my birthday, I moved our little
fire pit out into the middle of the lawn at our house to a spot where the
grass had turned dormant and dry. To help start the fire, I went into the
garage to look for some spare wood and selected an old, broken down
drawer that was obviously worthless and beyond repair.

As I threw it onto the fire, the kids came out and added some
branches to stoke the blaze. *It doesn't get much better than this,* I thought
to myself. Suddenly, everything changed! One of the branches that Wade
put on the fire fell onto the ground and ignited the dormant grass. I
imagined the fire quickly spreading to the porch and burning down the
house! We sprang into action; the three youngest and I ran around in a
panic, deciding on the fly to start filling cups of water from the kitchen
sink to pour them on the fire. "That's a good idea!" I shouted. Elijah
calmly found the hose, turned on the water, and put out the fire. *Why
didn't I think of that?* Wade felt horrible, but I assured him that everything was fine.

We all took some deep breaths, shared some nervous laughter, and
resumed our leisurely evening around the fire that was now thankfully
confined to the fire pit. Then my cell phone rang. It was kind of disturb-
ing my peaceful evening, but I noticed it was someone from the church.

I took the call. While I was on the phone, Linda came outside to join everyone. When she got about ten feet away from us I noticed her entire face change from peace and contentment to horror—and then anger.

"Who put that drawer—my antique drawer!—in the fire?!"

For the second time inside of ten minutes I transitioned from relaxing calm to incredible fear. My mind raced to the possible options before me. Actually, the most powerful temptation that I gave serious consideration to was something along the lines of, *You know, the kids have probably done lots of things that they should have received punishment and didn't. Perhaps I should let them take the fall for this?* The look on Linda's face convinced me that I had to step up, be a man, and admit my mistake. Our children's lives might be at stake! With more than a little fear and trepidation, I cupped my hand over the phone, quickly said, "It was me," and then went back to my conversation as though it was the most important phone call I'd received all year. In this case, it probably was!

Linda glared at me, turned on her heels, and went inside. I extended the discussion an extra few minutes, just to buy some time. I ran out of things to talk about, so I reluctantly said good-bye and hung up the phone. I waited another five minutes or so, but Linda did not return.

Unable to delay the inevitable any longer, I looked at my children for what could be the last time. I wanted to remember them just as they were. Then I courageously went to find Linda. She was in the garage. I could tell because through the walls I could hear her talking. "Who doesn't know not to burn antiques? Look at all of the other wood in here he could've chosen. Are you kidding me! What is wrong with him?"

I decided it best to leave her alone and let her work it out of her system. She seemed to be doing a pretty good job. I returned to the fire pit with the kids, happy to be reunited. Wade was still feeling really bad about setting the lawn on fire. I leaned over to him and said, "Trust me, son, *no one* is going to remember you setting the lawn on fire. My torching your mom's antique is the only thing we're going to remember from this night."

Eventually Linda came back out and joined us around the fire pit.

Her expression was sullen, her mouth tight lipped. Using my keen powers of perception, I could tell she was still a little upset. She peered into the blaze. Truth be told, I thought the antique drawer was burning quite nicely. I kept that thought to myself.

"Uh, I'm really sorry, hon," I said quietly.

"Yeah," she said in a measured tone. "I was saving that drawer because I was going to repair it."

I was confused. "But it had fallen apart. I mean, there weren't even any nails that I could see."

She took a deep breath, slowly let it out, raised her eyes to mine, and said in the most controlled voice she could muster, "Well, some of the best antique furniture doesn't have nails. They used glue."

"Ohhh." Ignorance is bliss? Not in this case! I had no idea. I didn't realize the value of the drawer or how easily it could be restored.

The same is true with us. We don't understand how valuable we are to God. The rest of the world may look at us and think we're not worth much. We may even agree, but our Heavenly Father sees something beautiful; someone priceless. And He is right! We are His children, adopted at a great price! Likewise, it doesn't take much for Him to repair us. He restores our souls. It is what He does when we *let* Him. That's why humility before God is everything! Through the power and wisdom of the Holy Spirit, it is astonishing how quickly God can heal us—and begin turning around any ministry. It doesn't happen all at once, but the Lord will bring the miraculous change if we don't quit on Him. It starts with admitting how broken we truly are and how much we truly need Him.

Family will help. They know.

They were the greatest miracles in the Bible!
Are you ready to stop chasing miracles so the
Spirit can make you miraculous? He hopes so. We all do!

When Linda told me, "Moe, I don't know if you will ever be happy," it was an unmistakable wake-up call to my brokenness. It was pointless to deny this fact anymore. I was only lying to myself, and not very well. I was looking for love in all the wrong places. I was looking for peace in all the wrong places. I was looking for significance in all the wrong places. I called out to God. Then it was simply a matter of repenting to come back to my first love, my Lord and Savior Jesus, rededicating my life and ministry to Him on a daily basis, restructuring my life and our ministries so the most important thing we *all* do is patiently listen to the Lord, refocusing on broken, hurting, helpless and precious people, and then simply rejoicing as the Spirit is unleashed to do what only the Spirit can do.

Consider Christ's first followers: ordinary men and women who stayed with Him. They listened and followed, listened and followed, listened and followed—and once they were filled with the Holy Spirit, God changed the world through them. *They* were the greatest miracles in the Bible! Are you ready to stop chasing miracles so the Spirit can make *you* miraculous? He hopes so. We all do!

You matter more than you know and to more people than you know. Maybe you've been like Martha, distracted with much serving, worried and troubled about many things. Jesus understands. Perhaps you are ready to become more like Mary, who learned to do the only necessary thing. Listen as the Prince of Peace speaks to you. Allow Him to quiet your spirit and speak to the deepest part of your soul. He loves you just the way you are. He always has. Allow Him to fill you with all the love you will ever need, and then He will lead you to people you *get* to lovingly pour into. Your life is no longer about you. It is about Him and them. He has work for you to do until He calls you home to heaven. The work is never alone. It is always *with* Him; and the two of you yoked together, serving the least and the lost, and giving God all the glory? "Oooooh boy!" as our brother in Christ John would say.

The Lord gets all the glory, so He gets the last word. I invite you to *slowly* read these words as though for the first time:

The Lord is my shepherd; I shall not want.
He makes me lie down in green pastures.
He leads me beside still waters.
He restores my soul.
He leads me in paths of righteousness for his name's sake.
Even though I walk through the valley of the shadow of death,
I will fear no evil, for you are with me; your rod and your staff,
they comfort me.
You prepare a table before me in the presence of my enemies;
you anoint my head with oil; my cup overflows.
Surely goodness and mercy shall follow me all the days of my life,
and I shall dwell in the house of the Lord forever.
Psalm 23

47580974R00104

Made in the USA
San Bernardino, CA
03 April 2017